Contents

Introduction v

one Testing times 1

two Right attitudes 24

three Accuracy tests 35

four Intelligence tests 37

five Personality tests 69

six Tests of creativity 87

seven Tests of attitude 98

eight Business games and role-playing 114

nine Practice makes perfect 130

ten Success and failure 149

Useful addresses 152

Index 154

Introduction

'Tests make me sweat'

Agnes and George have been living together for six months. They're an ambitious pair. She works as a PA to the managing director of a property development company. Boyfriend George wants to get into the glamorous world of TV production. He's been told he has to start at the bottom, and the bottom means working shifts at a company which copies tapes, CDs and DVDs. It's about as creative as mixing cement.

Both Agnes and George are fed up with their jobs. It's something they often moan about when they get home.

Agnes' boss isn't the most organized property developer in East London and he's got a tongue on him. He knows that people who work for him have nicknamed his company 'In a Panic Properties Ltd'. He's always not meeting deadlines and he can never find the documents he needs. He expects Agnes to sort out the swamp that is central filing, and sweet talk the building inspectors. The pressure is beginning to worry her. She's too scared to ask if she can take a long weekend so that she and George can go rambling in the Lake District.

George is not pressured but he is bored. He has a degree in media studies and saw himself becoming a TV chat show host. Instead, he's doing a job which most robots would consider beneath them.

'And they'd have to pay a robot more,' he joshes.

'Why don't you change your job?' Agnes suggests.

'Why don't you change yours?' George flips back.

Agnes can't decide whether to try for that or not. There is no chance of getting a reference from her boss because it's just not the kind of thing he does. Also she is a news junkie, and all the papers forecast that towards the end of the year the world will be facing hard times. The price of oil is sky high; jobs are going to the cheap labour economies of the Far East. Inflation and rising unemployment loom. If she quits her job, it may not be that easy to get a new job that is better than 'In a Panic'. And Agnes hates the thought of going back to temping.

Agnes' second reason is a bit personal and awkward. She manages to act more confident than she is. She does not have a degree in media studies like George; she has some mediocre GCSEs and her shorthand is nothing to write home about. She is nervous that she would have a hard time getting a new job because she knows it would mean taking tests. One blessing of 'In a Panic Properties' was that as soon as her boss saw she could read, write, add up and answer the phone, he hired her. There was no question of Agnes having to take IQ, personality or attitude tests.

Most employers, she knows, aren't so Neanderthal.

She also knows that many PAs would never put up with her boss, and she figures that in six months' time she will be the only person who understands the filing system – and so she can ask for a raise. If she dares.

So Agnes says to George, 'It could be worse.'

So she will put up with a job she really is fed up with because she is anxious she would fail any normal recruitment process.

George, on the other hand, is not nervous of tests at all, but he is careless. He has not told Agnes that he keeps going for jobs and not getting them. Since he got a decent degree and thinks of himself as smart and witty, he assumes he is over-qualified and doesn't ever ask for feedback from companies that turn him down. As a result, George has no idea where he's going wrong – and no hope of improving his prospects.

What will happen when Agnes finds out George is not so smart?

And what will happen when George finds out Agnes suffers from psycho-test phobia?

It's time to end this mini soap opera and to start, since the title of this book is *How to Succeed in Psychometric Tests*!

1. **Testing times**

It's hardly surprising people wonder – and sometimes worry – about psychometric tests. A survey in 1996 by the Industrial Relations Service found that 87.3 per cent of large and medium-sized British companies used some form of psychometric test when hiring people.

In the last ten years in the West people have been tested more and more. Employers want to be sure that the people they are hiring can do the job and will stay on the job. Every time a company has to hire someone new it costs money.

And the British government encourages the process by testing children on junior versions of many of the tests discussed in this book. I recently found the following advice for parents on a government website:

Preparing Your Child for Testing

Preparing your child for psychoeducational testing can reduce anxiety and encourage cooperation through the upcoming battery of tests. One practice is to introduce the discussion by the number of days as the child is old; if the child is eight years old, discuss the evaluation at least eight days in advance of the testing. Reassure your child that the reason for testing is to understand why school is a struggle despite hard work and attempts to do well. Explain that the tests will contain a variety of questions, puzzles, drawings, stories, and games; and that the tests are neither painful nor about whether the child is crazy. Most importantly, offer the child hope in that the evaluation should show adults how best to help. Be open and honest as much as possible.

When it comes to testing adults, psychologists and employers certainly could be far more open about the complexities and uses of testing. It's not hard, however, to guess why they are not. Testing gives employers and recruitment agencies great power over people who want jobs or who are being assessed for promotion within an organization.

There are ethical codes of practice for giving tests but these codes are very polite and utterly voluntary. The British Psychological Society, for example, 'expects' those who give tests to behave fairly. There is no legal force behind the guidelines. They are what employers call 'best practice'.

Psychometric tests have many uses and some tests have considerable scientific validity. But they are also part of a game – the game where you are looking for work from companies and they want to see if you are going to be useful to them. It's very easy to worry that mega-brained probe-psychologists with their laser-beam insights are going to see through to the depths of your soul. Tests are revealing but they are not Superman's X-ray vision – there are more things than Kryptonite which tests can't probe.

However, testing remains something they do to you.

And managers even admit this. In replies to the 2001 and 2002 Recruitment Survey run by the Chartered Institute of Personnel Management, they admitted taking more control of the testing process. Of the tests the managers used, 60 per cent examined general abilities and 4 per cent personality.

But you are not powerless.

The best way to cope is to know as much as possible about what tests are like, how to handle them and how to manage the very natural anxieties people have about them. My aim in this book is to provide a practical and up-to-date guide so you will be fully prepared to take just about any test any employer will present you with.

What can you do to do justice to yourself in tests?

- Understand.
- Analyse.
- Practise.

The more you know about how tests are designed and marked, the more chance you have of doing that. Tests often have traps or trick questions which are designed to shed light on inconsistencies or weaknesses.

In this book I'm often critical of tests, but there are good reasons for their popularity with employers. One of the most solid findings of psychology over the last century is that simply interviewing people to decide whether or not they will do a job well is not enough. Human beings – i.e. the interviewers – are not very objective. We tend to pick the person we like best or, in some cases, the one who will threaten us least. Sometimes personnel officers even pick the candidate they think is the most physically attractive. Looking good is no guarantee of doing the job well, however, or Claudia Schiffer would be General Secretary of the United Nations. Uglies or those who are more aesthetically challenged, take heart!

Precisely because they are more objective, psychometric tests have become more and more central to recruitment at every level. In Britain and in America, every major employer from the Civil Service to Sainsbury's to Marks and Spencer uses them to recruit. Some big companies are going even further. The supermarket chain Asda have just announced that they are doing their best to automate their recruitment process – i.e. people will do tests on the internet. Huggies, the health care company who make Kleenex, have also said they are going to use testing more and more.

The British Psychological Society now lists over 45 publishers of tests in the UK. It has been estimated that the industry is worth £500 million in the United Kingdom and over $1 billion in the United States.

And there are plenty of tests employers can choose from. One well-respected textbook lists over 8,000 tests on the market, ranging from IQ tests to the 'How Good a Salesman Are You?' test to the Marital Satisfaction Index to the Intercollegiate Basketball Instrument, a wonderful paper and pencil test which reveals whether you play basketball well or not. You don't have to touch or pass a ball for the psychologist to know. I especially like a new 2007 Filial Piety Test which tells Mexicans whether or not they are good sons. There are enough tests on the market for an American publisher, Pro Ed of Austin, Texas, to publish 11 volumes – each about 500 pages long – dedicated solely to describing tests and offering a critique of each of them.

Despite the spread of tests, there are some interesting

exceptions to the rule that you need to do well at psychometric tests to get a job. You do not have to pass such tests to become an accountant, a doctor, a lawyer. As long as you pass the relevant academic exams, you get that -ology and you are qualified. You also do not have to take a psychometric test to become a Member of Parliament. That may be as well, since much research suggests that politicians suffer from a variety of personality quirks. Also, there is now a vogue for integrity tests which reveal whether you lie and how much you can be trusted. How well would politicians do on them?

Psychometric tests for MPs – well, it's a nice idea but I somehow suspect MPs will never vote for it.

The internet

One fact you have to face is that testing keeps changing.

In the past, recruitment involved tests in two ways. Step 1 was always the same – you made a job application. The company decided whether or not you were suitable based on your qualifications and previous job experience. The CV was key.

Step 2 in the past tended to be screening, where a specific test was given to highlight those who might be worth interviewing. Companies often were quite picky. But that was before the internet changed the process of testing, which it has done radically over the last five years.

According to Dave Bartram, who was Professor of Psychology at Hull University before joining SHL, one of Britain's largest test companies: 'One of the most fundamental changes has been the internet. In the past you had to do tests on paper and pencil and those were quite costly.'

They were costly because each candidate had to be scored individually by a member of staff. Now the internet does it all. You are sent a questionnaire or a test, you fill it in online, and email it back.

In the past each booklet had to be scored individually and that was expensive in terms of time and money. Now companies can give tests on the internet in a format which allows replies to be scored automatically. So the process of scoring the tests becomes cheap, and now companies and recruitment agencies use them earlier in the process – to 'pre-sift' candidates.

'You are more likely to be asked to do a psychometric test earlier in the recruitment process because it is easier to sift these results online – and cheaper,' Bartram told me. And he is himself the author of a learned tome called *Computer-Based Testing and the Internet* (2003).

What was once a tool – and not the main one – in choosing who to hire has now become the most important part of the process. If your test profile is not what the company wants, you are unlikely ever to be seen by their personnel officers.

'The internet has also made it easier to vary tests so that those who are going to take them can no longer cram and copy what they find. There are fewer standardized questions,' Bartram added.

That means it is easier for companies to tailor tests to their own individual needs.

The consequences of the fact that more and more testing will be done on the internet cannot be over-estimated. You will need to have good computer skills and must conquer any fears of technology if you want to do well.

When I asked Professor Bartram about concerns with testing, he was quite optimistic. Testing worked well. But is that how people who take tests feel? Not entirely.

The employment agency Reed Consulting recently carried out a survey of 8,000 people who had gone through the recruitment process. Of these, 37 per cent said that the most useful part was work simulation exercises, in which they were asked to do tasks very similar to those they would have to do if they got the job. Another 23 per cent said interviews were the most useful part of the process. But many of the subjects sniped that they didn't understand the purpose of the psychometric tests they were asked to do. It seemed the most baffling part of the process.

But that hasn't stopped the testing business refining and developing more and more tests, obvious tests a dim-witted elephant could see through and cunning subtle ones you need to be on guard for.

New tests

Every day, in every way, new tests are being dreamed up – and, in theory, tested. The Myers Briggs test – of which more later – has become probably the most used test in the world. Two more much used new tests we will review are the Graduate Management Admission Test and the Decision Analysis Test.

Some researchers have also started to develop tests of the dark side of your work personality. You can look forward to being asked if, when you are under stress at work, the vampire in you comes out – the Stephen King test.

One of the things employers have always wanted to know is how reliable and how honest recruits might be. But for 100 years personality tests did not try to answer these questions. It was seen as just too difficult, so for the first century of psychology I don't think there was a 'How Much of a Liar Are You?' test.

But now there are both overt and covert integrity tests. Overt tests ask openly if you often tell lies. If you are a habitual liar, you will lie, of course, and say you never tell lies. Covert integrity tests are more subtle because they do not openly ask such questions directly. No organization wants to hire someone dishonest, because they may steal and skive, but clearly there are some jobs in which honesty really matters – the police, for one.

Today every single police force in the United Kingdom makes would-be recruits do some form of integrity testing. The *Report on Police Integrity* (2003), Personnel and Training section 5.2, states that:

> Greater use could be made during recruitment of assessment centres, with integrity being tested through the dynamics of group discussions and scenario testing. It is important then to feed in information from such testing, together with whatever knowledge has been gained of the applicant's actual previous conduct, to a rigorous but fairly conducted final interview. A potential weak spot, therefore, is in using staff without proven interview skills; there is a mistaken belief that the skills required for interviewing offenders are the same. One chief constable aptly describes his recruiting department as 'the bouncers for my ballroom'. An ethos should be

generated within those departments that they are of immense importance to the maintenance of integrity within the Service.

I'm not entirely sure whether the psychologists would like to be seen as bouncers. But the report makes it clear that it is not simple to work out how much of a liar someone is. And calling his recruitment department 'bouncers' tells us something about that Chief Constable.

Senior jobs

Once, it would have been considered bad manners to give a psychological test to someone applying for a senior job. That has changed completely. Rosemary Moore, senior consultant at Capita Ras, who have handled much hiring for the British Civil Service, told me in 1998, 'Tests are becoming accepted even in recruiting very high-level jobs. People expect them to be part of the process.' Clients love them.

When it comes to high-level jobs, tests become even more sophisticated. You do not just get tests of IQ and personality and integrity, but role-playing and in-tray exercises, not to mention 360° assessments.

But there is one interesting exception to all this, as I discovered when a charity of which I am a trustee had to appoint a new Head of Finance and a new Chief Executive.

Fifteen of us sit round the board table of the charity. We have to choose two of the key people who will run an organization that has over 500 staff, a number of hostels and sheltered housing. The turnover is around 20 million a year – and it should be higher.

If we were just running Sell as Many Widgets as Possible Ltd, we would be looking for 'leaders' whose job would be to make as big a profit as possible. Of course, Widget 'Supremo' would also have to keep up with cutting-edge widget technology and make sure the streamlined widget production process was as slick as possible.

But this is a charity, and while we have to make money we also have values we want to promote and campaigns we want to run. This will make the recruiting complicated.

We decide we must hire headhunters who will help us find good candidates and test them.

And here we come to a paradox. There is no test I know of which allows you to test how well headhunters hunt heads. You have to rely on company histories (the corporate equivalent of CVs) and the interviewing and pitching process. There's a bit of irony here, given that headhunters are part of the recruitment business.

This book is an attempt to redress the balance, to give people who have to take tests some insight into what the whole process is about. I include specific exercises which will allow you to analyse and improve your skills. One device I have included to help is a Balance Sheet of the Self, of your strengths and weaknesses. This is on pages 134–8. Don't fill it in yet. Wait until you get to chapter 2 by which time you will understand exactly what it tries to do.

TIPS

Throughout the book I offer very specific tips on how to handle particular tests. Many of these tips are pure common sense. Others are based on an understanding of what those who give tests are looking for – and think they are looking for. None of the tips are absolute. You need to read them carefully and work out which ones are the most help for you.

Before 1855, people got jobs in the Civil Service in Britain if they had the right connections. Ability did not come into it. If you were the second son of Lord Silverspoon or the cousin of Sir Plutocrat, you had all the necessary qualifications. No further questions needed.

Victorian reformers decided that this was not entirely fair. The best man – there really was no question about the 'best woman' then – might not get the job. Sir Charles Trevelyan introduced entry examinations for the Civil Service and the government argued that Britain would from now on be administered by very able people.

Sir Charles Trevelyan's tests were academic rather than

psychological; they owed a great deal to the final examinations at Oxford and Cambridge. Nevertheless, they were an important break with tradition. For the first time ever in Britain, candidates had to prove they were suitable for a job.

Trevelyan was not the first to think of using examinations to select the best candidates for government jobs. The Chinese emperors used literary examinations to choose recruits for the Imperial Service in the Middle Ages. Nevertheless, the Victorians were very proud of their democratic innovation.

Both the Chinese and the British assumed that someone who could write elegant essays – or verses – would also be able to administer a government department well. Until the 1960s, an optional paper in the British Civil Service exam was Latin verse composition. If you could write Latin poetry that was a passable imitation of Virgil, you could run the country well. It stood to reason.

The reason I am being ironic is that, of course, it does not stand to reason at all. History is full of examples of people who have failed in exams and done very well in life. It is also full of people who have done brilliantly in exams and then achieved nothing else.

Winston Churchill was a failure at school. In his autobiography he wrote that he did poorly in all his examinations. The interesting thing about this is that he was not just a fine politician who saved the world – the kind of task that exams do not really help predict performance in – but he was also a fine writer. He earned his living by his pen from his early twenties. Writing well, you would imagine, is the kind of skill that could be predicted from performance in tests and examinations.

A second example is just as startling. The great physicist Albert Einstein initially failed to enter the University of Zurich. He had to take a lowly job as a clerk at the Zurich Patent Office. It was while he was basically an engineering pen-pusher that he hit on the ideas and experiments which revolutionized physics.

Many historians of science argue that if Einstein had had a conventional education in physics, he would never have discovered the theory of relativity. As an outsider, he could challenge orthodox physics. If he had passed his exams, he would have been much less interesting, possibly just another routine scientist.

The late Hans Eysenck, the eminent psychologist who stoutly defended intelligence testing for most of his career, told me in the 1990s that he was only too aware of the limits of the tests. He was specially sceptical of Mensa, the club you can join only if you have an IQ of 140 – which roughly five people out of every 1,000 have. Eysenck liked to point out that the only achievement many members of Mensa can boast of is their high IQ.

If high IQ doesn't mean money, fame or happiness, then what is it worth? It is significant that some members of Mensa are themselves becoming critical of IQ as a measure of a person's value.

In October 1998, Julie Baxter, until recently the head of Mensa in the UK, told its annual conference high IQ was not the only quality that mattered either in life or in work. She waxed lyrical about the merits of 'emotional maturity' and 'goodwill' – and then resigned.

Some financial scandals also make one wonder about the merits of IQ. Late in 1998, Long Term Credit, an American management hedge fund which invested on the basis of equations developed by two Nobel laureates, lost so much money that international banks had to bail them out to the tune of $3.5 billion. Pundits claim the world's financial system might have been in danger of collapse if Long Term Credit had gone under. The super-brainy equations didn't quite work.

I'm not sure anyone tested the IQ of the brains behind Long Term Credit but it seems reasonable to assume that Nobel Prize winners aren't short of IQ.

Many of us like to believe such stories. They are comforting: if you fail tests, you might still turn out to be Churchill or Einstein. But they also embody a truth that is worth remembering: *tests can only test so much.*

For almost a century, psychologists have quarrelled about how useful tests are. Some believe that they really can predict performance in all kinds of skills, as long as they are interpreted intelligently. Other, equally expert psychologists warn that most of the tests currently in use promise more than they predict. They look objective but, in fact, are far from accurate in predicting how well individuals will perform.

Psychological tests started to be used widely during the

1914–18 war. Both the British and the American armies needed a quick way to sort out recruits into those who were able, those who needed a great deal of training and those who were more of a threat to their troops than to the enemy. The armed forces had to weed out hopeless cases. American historians of psychology now accept that much of the information initially obtained from these tests was inaccurate. For example, they 'proved' Jews and Italians had specially low IQs.

The first study that led to the development of proper tests was started in France in 1904. The Paris education authorities wanted to find out how they could improve the lot of children who were doing badly at school. They commissioned two psychologists, Alfred Binet and Theodore Simon, to study the problem. Binet and Simon studied what children could achieve at different ages and established what was normal for children to achieve from the age of two upwards.

Binet and Simon developed two measures. First, a normal measure of what a child should be able to manage at a particular age. Second, ways of testing the abilities of any individual child.

It was out of this work that the notion of IQ was born. The Intelligence Quotient is mental age (what an individual child can achieve) divided by what is normal for children as a whole at that age.

This work, which had excellent liberal motives, was soon taken up by the military who wanted to keep out of the army recruits who were positively useless.

Many of the questions the military wanted answered are the kinds of questions that interest employers. They include:

• How intelligent is this person?
• Can they follow orders?
• What kind of skills do they have?
• Are they adaptable?
• How do they react under pressure?
• Do they have leadership qualities?

It was the success of tests used by the military in the 1914–18 war that made industry interested. From 1921, the Psychological Corporation in America offered companies advice on how to use psychology to recruit new workers. In Britain there was a similar organization called the National Board for Occupational Psychology. Psychological tests are now used by employers in Britain, America, Japan and Europe. Increasingly, they are also used to monitor the progress of employees. Career development involves the use of more psychological tests than ever before.

The *Mental Tests Yearbook* of 2006 notes that in this questionnaire-blessed year over 220 new tests reached the market. Some of these tests were not job-related, and included 15 new IQ tests, 31 new achievement tests and 15 new vocational tests. Astonishingly, it did not include my new favourite the Filial Piety in Mexico Test. The *Yearbook* runs to 1150 pages.

As publishers rush helter-skelter into what seems to be a profitable market, many tests are being offered without the slightest evidence of attempts to verify if they predict how well people will do in jobs.

Interesting examples of this trend are the Sales Style Indicator which allegedly reveals what kind of salesman or woman you might be and the Small Business Assessment which will uncover whether you have the personality to fit in well in a small company. The Sales Style Indicator has only 16 questions but these are enough apparently to tell whether you've got the assertive gifts needed to sell snow to Eskimos as well as the human skills to score high on Interpersonal Harmony.

Types of test

In the following pages I give many examples of questions from different kinds of tests. IQ tests ask questions to which there are definite answers. But tests of attitudes of various kinds come in different formats. In some tests you will be asked to give a simple YES/NO:

Do you enjoy meeting people? YES/NO

This makes such tests easy to score but they are often infuriating because you really want to say 'Maybe' or 'Sometimes'.

A little more room for manoeuvre is provided by Scale Tests. They will ask you to rate how well you agree with this statement:

I do not like travelling to remote areas

A five-point scale will offer five different responses: Agree Strongly, Agree, No View, Disagree, Disagree Strongly. A seven-point scale allows for more subtlety: Agree Strongly, Agree, Tend to Agree, No View, Tend to Disagree, Disagree, Disagree Strongly.

TIP

Be careful about marking too many extreme scores at the end of each scale. The instructions for some tests warn that while people who always choose the middle ranks are indecisive, those who consistently choose either Strongly Agree or Strongly Disagree are impulsive and exhibitionist. This is especially true with seven-point scales.

A third form of test asks you to tick a number of words that best describe your view of a statement like:

The most important thing you need to succeed is
- drive
- the willingness to learn
- originality
- obeying company instructions
- not wasting time chattering in the office.

Always be careful to check the precise instructions that go with the question. Clearly all these five can contribute to a well-run company but often the test insists you pick just one. Pick more and it looks as though you are unwilling to listen and cannot follow instructions.

Remember, tests are devised partly for the convenience of those who score them. You have, to some extent, to live by their rules, though I hope to give you some good tips on how not to be browbeaten by them.

Open-ended questions

One of the trickiest problems is open-ended questions. They look friendly, a chance to express yourself, but they also demand great concentration. Usually, they ask complicated questions about such things as why you want the job, what you have to contribute and where you hope to be five years from now in career terms.

Each of these questions has dangers:

- *Why do you want this job?* You need to be enthusiastic but not fawning. You also need to be concise. No one wants to read a three-page essay.
- *What do you have to contribute?* You must obviously sell yourself but you have to do so intelligently. Do not rave on about being the greatest bookkeeper in the world. If you are going for a job as a salesman, bring in any figures you have about sales you have achieved.
- *Where do you want to be five years from now?* That is really tricky. Too much ambition may actually frighten your interviewers; too little makes you look like you won't pull your weight.

So the best way to deal with spontaneous open-ended questions is to have worked out beforehand in detail your answers, so that you can make a credible but not over-the-top pitch about why you want the job and what you can do.

The usefulness of tests

Tests are popular because they are backed, in theory, by the authority of science. When a personnel department uses a test they assume it has been properly tried out and developed through a process of trial and error. The test will be valid and reliable. Validity and reliability are technical concepts that it is important for someone trying to understand tests to grasp.

Reliability means that if I take a test on Monday or Thursday, I will score more or less the same. Results that individuals achieve should not fluctuate dramatically. This is usually true with good tests of IQ and of some personality traits. It is much less true of tests that ask you to choose your favourite design or colours. An unreliable test is not much use.

The validity of a test is harder to show. A test is valid if it actually tests what it claims to test. It is easy to give an example of an invalid test. I do very well on the Columbia Driver

Judgment Test which sets paper and pencil questions about how to drive a heavy goods vehicle round New York. Unfortunately, I cannot drive. I failed my driving test on 17 counts the first time I took it. When preparing for my second test, I crashed the Mini I was driving into Guildford Town Hall. At this point, I decided that as far as motor cars went I had better just be a passenger. My experience suggests that the Columbia Driver Judgment Test is not testing driving skill. Rather, what the test is tapping is spatial ability.

Reliable and valid tests are useful. They offer rapid information about would-be employees. They are also popular because a large body of research shows that interviews by themselves are not very reliable as a method of selection. People's judgements are often very subjective: whether they like the look of someone counts for more than almost anything else. Unfortunately, however, very few tests are really reliable or valid.

The fact that tests claim to be objective makes many people anxious. Will the test reveal aspects of my personality that are bad, that I don't want to give away? Will it show up defects I don't know myself? Many of us think psychology is largely about unlocking secrets – often guilty secrets. It is also worrying if someone is judging you and has information on you you don't have yourself.

Some psychologists – and the techniques they use – encourage this mystique. Look at the illustration below. It is an inkblot. What does it look like to you? There is a huge amount of technical literature on this Rorschach test which claims to be able to deduce all kinds of aspects of your personality depending on whether you think the blob is a turtle, a helmet or a hillock.

There are ways of testing people which make it possible to overcome such anxieties but often psychologists are not sensitive enough to use them.

Tests are curious. They provoke anxiety and fascination. Hundreds of magazines publish tests of all kinds on whether you are a great lover, on whether you have a seductive sense of humour, whether you have what it takes to become a tycoon or stick to a low calorie diet. In a book I co-authored with Douglas Shelley, *Testing Psychological Tests,* we found that newspapers as up-market as the *Sunday Times* carried tests regularly in the belief that they attracted readers.

But the test you decide to do in *Marie Claire* or *Esquire* is very different from the test you take for a job. Most magazine tests do not take themselves too seriously. Nothing is at stake. It is a game, almost a piece of self-indulgence. You spend a little time answering questions, often questions about yourself. How nice! If you do not like the answers or they do not seem accurate, few readers take it to heart. It is a bit of a joke, and a game where you are in control.

Taking a serious test is not the same. You are not in control. There are no answers you can look up. If the questions seem irrelevant, there is little you can do about it. One study of how people felt about tests (by a Polish psychologist) showed that 17 per cent of questions seemed to be trivial and 21 per cent irrelevant. The study also discovered that many people found particular questions threatening. Perhaps worst of all, many people felt that taking a test was like doing a school examination. Both are *tests* after all. In theory, it should not be so.

One of my aims in this book is to give readers some sense of being in control so that you do not feel that being tested is something that is only being done *to* you.

Guidelines

One way to achieve a measure of control is to understand something of the process behind testing, to have available much of the information that psychologists and personnel officers have. Testing is unfortunately full of 'restrictive practices'.

Students who are preparing for exams can quite legitimately buy old exam papers. Ordinary people cannot, however, buy many psychological tests. Most reputable test publishers will only sell them to people they consider properly qualified. Often these qualifications are not academic but a function of the job you have. The motive for restricted selling is to protect people from rogue testing and to stop people preparing the answers! In effect, the restrictions contribute to the mystique. Only the really learned can possess the precious tests. The rest are locked out from 'The Knowledge'. Only a few popular books like Eysenck's *Test Your Own IQ* offer any kind of reliable information.

Both the British Psychological Society (BPS) and the much larger American Psychological Association (APA) are worried about the way testing is being carried out. The BPS in its guidelines says that there is so much poor testing going on in the UK that the very procedure of testing is being brought into disrepute. The BPS and the APA are concerned that individuals are made to feel insecure by the process of testing. The BPS notes that 'tests are often offered as a panacea or ultimate solution' when they are, in reality, at best a useful tool in choosing people for jobs.

Despite the fact that few tests can be bought on the open market, one fact that worries both the BPS and the APA is that many of those in industry who administer tests are not really qualified to do so. Not to mince matters, they do not know what they are doing.

The BPS guidelines point out that at present four kinds of people administer tests. The first two are:

- well-trained psychologists;
- psychologists who are qualified but not properly trained in testing skills. A degree in psychology is not enough, as the courses in most UK universities do not cover many critical issues. To understand the mechanics of testing requires a good deal of technical knowledge about how tests are constructed and also a lot of seemingly difficult statistics.

In reality, as the BPS acknowledges, tests are often given by people with no psychological training at all. The BPS divides these into:

- non-psychologists who have a good deal of training in testing. Qualified personnel officers are the most likely to fall into this group. They are, in theory, the least likely to do harm;
- non-psychologists who are not properly trained but who find themselves in a job where they are assumed to be fit to give tests. Such people can do a lot of damage in administering tests − both to the companies that employ them and to the individuals to whom they give tests.

The BPS stresses that tests 'should not be imposed'. When someone takes a test, ideally it should be seen as a co-operative effort between the test-giver and the test-taker. Co-operation sounds nice but the situations in which people take tests are usually competitive. The personnel department have jobs or promotion to offer and the candidate wants the job or promotion. It really is not an enterprise between equals. I do not see any way of getting round this; it reflects who has power and who does not.

In America, psychologists are far more influential and better organized than in Britain. Nevertheless, their professional organizations have only been marginally more successful in controlling the standards of tests and test administration.

To deal with the problem of badly given tests, the BPS set up a scheme in January 1991 to qualify people to administer tests. This Certificate of Competences in Operational Testing is available to people who can show they are competent in:

- defining assessment needs
- basic principles of scaling and standardization (scaling is the technical term for whether tests ask you to rate on 1−3, 1−5 or 1−7 how you feel or think. The kind of scale affects how results should be interpreted)
- reliability and validity
- deciding when a test should be used
- administering and scoring tests
- making appropriate use of test results
- maintaining security and confidentiality.

In 1995, amendments to the guidelines were brought in to allow one set of chartered psychologists to verify how other psychologists were giving and supervising tests. The BPS also had just brought in a new certificate for people who give personality as opposed to aptitude tests.

This initiative is a step forward and there is no doubt that the BPS recognizes an important problem. But their solution leaves much to be desired.

The British Psychological Society (BPS) has produced both question-and-answer booklets on testing and a Code of Good Practice, as it gets many questions about testing from the public. The booklets have their own ironies, however, as the questions they deal with seem much more likely to come from those who want to become testers than from ordinary job seekers who have to take tests. One question in the booklets asks what you have to do to get on the Register of Competence in Occupational Testing. Unless the job you want is giving tests to people, the answers to that question are not likely to be much help.

Despite all these anxieties, the Code of Good Practice brought out by the BPS in 2002 is short and rather basic.

People who use psychological tests for assessment are expected by the BPS to take steps to ensure they are able to meet all the standards of competence. They are also expected not to exaggerate their skills – i.e. fib – and not to offer services which lie outside their sphere of competence. They are asked to respect the confidentiality of clients and to make sure test results are stored securely

The items dedicated to client welfare are again rather basic. They include:

Obtain the informed consent of potential test-takers or their legitimate representatives making sure they understand why the tests will be used, what will be done with the results and who will have access to them.

Ensure that all test-takers are well informed and well prepared for the test session and that all have had access to practice or familiarization.

Provide the test-taker or authorized persons with feedback.

Give due considerations to factors such as gender, disability, ethnicity, age and special needs.

Finally, the testers are supposed to make sure that the tests are not used for any purpose other than that agreed with the test-taker.

Of course, the guidelines do not mention the internet. There is nothing wrong with these guidelines in themselves, and the recruitment industry says they are generally respected, but frankly there is no evidence either way.

Also, we don't really know what sanctions there are against those who break these gentlemen's rules!

The BPS also publishes a non-evaluative list of test publishers. Being non-evaluative, the list does not reveal which publishers are reputable and which dreamed up their tests on a wet afternoon when they had nothing else to do. Fifteen of the publishers listed produce tests of ability such as IQ tests but 25 publish tests of personality and motivation. These tests are far less reliable than IQ ones.

Publishers do sometimes warn that personality and motivation tests are more useful in career guidance or as part of internal assessment procedures but the evidence is that employers often don't pay much attention. Test publishers rarely refuse to sell tests to people whose job – say as a personnel officer or a social worker – means they need them.

Sometimes the tests used seem odd, given the nature of the job vacancy. Sainsbury's, the supermarket chain, get applicants to fill in a Motivational Questionnaire. Many questions relate to how motivated you might feel about selling things to people. It is hard, however, to see how this kind of motivation matters. In a supermarket, the staff don't sell. They stack shelves, check stock, decide what products to put where. They interact with the public only if they work a cash till or if their job is to deal with complaints and enquiries.

Someone who hates the idea of selling might be rather good at the till or with complaints. Mr Motivated who gets a buzz when he makes a sale may actually hate working in a supermarket. But how many people applying for a job would dare say they hate the idea of selling things to the public?

Sainsbury's are far from unique. The problem is that many employers don't have the time or the expertise to master the complicated arguments about what tests can, or can't, achieve.

For those who have to take tests, independent advice is hard to get. There is no organization defending the rights of those who take tests.

Like the British Psychological Society, the Chartered Institute of Personnel and Development concentrates on providing information for companies and human resources staff. The Institute publishes a comprehensive guide; it covers the range of tests available and advises how to make sure tests are given in the most efficient and cost-effective way. It offers little to those who have to take tests to get a job.

If you can't get a job stacking shelves without doing a motivational test, you had better face facts.

You're not going to avoid tests if you want a job. Or if you want to keep a job. Many companies now also use tests to assess employees and decide where to move them in their organization.

For all these reasons, people need the best information on testing.

Vocational guidance

There is one long tradition in Britain of 'collaborative testing'. Organizations have offered vocational guidance for well over 50 years. The difference between being given tests as part of the job interview procedures and going for vocational guidance is stark. When you seek vocational guidance, you are the client. You are entitled to all the information that emerges.

Unemployed people can now get vocational guidance paid for by the Department of Employment. It can be very useful. A friend of mine had a thorough review which covered many options. He was surprised to hear he should look into becoming a funeral director. But the results showed he was good with people and not squeamish, two qualities that are useful in dealing both with corpses and with the bereaved.

Doing well in tests is largely a matter of attitude. Throughout the book I try to offer practical advice on how to handle various kinds of tests. The next chapter looks at how you should approach taking tests and what psychology can offer to make the whole process less of an ordeal.

The following five chapters look at particular kinds of tests that are much used. Chapter 4 looks at intelligence tests and, especially, at the different kinds of intelligence – verbal, visual, mathematical – that IQ tests measure. Employers want to know if a person has the right kind of intelligence for the job. It is no good appointing someone who is a verbal wizard to a job that needs manual dexterity.

Chapter 5 looks at personality tests, an area of great interest to employers. A salesman who lacks self-confidence and doesn't like talking to strangers is unlikely to do brilliantly. Many companies also use personality tests to see how employees will fit in. Is someone so much of a loner that, good as he or she is, they are likely to wreck the group?

Chapter 6 looks at tests of creativity. Many jobs, of course, are not remotely creative but in a society where presentation and handling information is more and more important, many jobs require some creativity. Can tests say much about that? Tests of creativity are much more controversial than tests of IQ and personality partly because creativity is much harder to define.

Chapter 7 looks at tests of motivation and attitude. How much does a person want to succeed? These tests, like tests of creativity, are much more controversial than IQ tests.

Chapter 8 looks at the role of business games and role-playing tests. These tests are used more and more by companies not just when they recruit but also when they want to monitor the progress of existing employees and decide how to improve their training.

Chapter 9 looks at two issues: how well practising for tests works and the linked question of what tests cannot test. Choosing someone for a job cannot usually be a scientific choice. For both employers and workers, the problem is made worse by the fact that you need to be well versed in the psychological literature to understand what tests can, and cannot, do. Some insecure personnel officers rely on tests because it gives them a good fall-back position. They can always say that he or she scored brilliantly on paper if it turns out that someone they hired is a disaster. The chapter advises caution on the part of personnel departments. Do not presume a test reveals more than the research on it indicates.

Chapter 10 sums up and advises on how to handle both success and failure in taking tests.

In every chapter, I try to indicate both the kinds of tests that may be given, some selected questions, and tips on how to deal with the problems that inevitably come up.

2. **Right attitudes**

In 1916, a famous psychologist called John Watson told his students that they had to draw up a 'balance sheet' of the self. They could not become practising psychologists, offering advice to other people, unless they understood their own strengths and weaknesses.

Watson was practical. He believed psychology should help ordinary people improve their lives. The more you knew about how and why you behaved, the more you could control your destiny − and change it if you wanted to.

Watson was one of the founders of The Psychological Corporation, a company that pioneered the use of tests by industry in America. Today, it still devises and assesses tests.

Watson had to deal with many reverses during his life. He was born dirt poor. His father ran away from home. Still, he managed to get to university and carve out a brilliant career until he had an affair with a student. In those moralistic times, he was sacked from his job. In his crisis, he used his knowledge of psychology − and himself − to survive. Three years after he was deeply depressed as a result of losing his professorship, Watson was a director of J. Walter Thompson, the advertising agency − and very rich.

I mention Watson because he believed people should be able to make use of psychology. When it comes to taking tests, there are a lot of general psychological principles which can help make it less of an ordeal, and almost enjoyable!

Every one of us is different so it would be silly to lay down a set of absolute ground rules for getting into the right frame of mind to be tested. Nevertheless, here are five aims you probably should have before you go into any testing:

- Feel relaxed. If you find this difficult, prepare by doing a little deep breathing and trying to clear your mind of any cluttering, tense thoughts.
- Make sure that you are well prepared.

- Get into a positive frame of mind. That doesn't mean being sure that you will get the job, which leaves you vulnerable to disappointment and depression. Feel determined to do justice to your abilities.
- Suppress any tendency you have to be either cocky or defensive.

and, crucially:

- Feel confident enough to ask about the things you don't understand about the process of being tested.

A psychological test is not an academic exam. The last thing you should feel is that this is like taking your GCSEs, A levels or finals. Some tests resemble exams but they do not really have the same aims. Do not bring into the process of being tested any hang-ups you may have left over from school or college.

At school, from the age of seven, we endlessly do exams; some are easy, some hard, some real, some mock. Teachers expect pupils to get used to the process. Any pupil knows that you cannot ask anyone to help out and that you must not cheat.

But, for most people, taking a test is a novel experience. You should not be expected to know the rules of this particular exercise. So, don't feel embarrassed about asking whoever is giving the test to clarify some important points like:

- what they hope the test will reveal;
- what they can tell you in advance about it;
- what they will tell you as feedback.

Exams judge whether or not particular candidates come up to particular standards. It doesn't interest the maths examiners if you happen to write English well. But any comprehensive psychological testing seeks a rounded picture of what you can and cannot do. It may also look at your personality, ambitions, your sense of self-confidence and your social skills. No academic exam is the slightest bit interested in these. Often, the aim of psychological testing is to arrive at a balance sheet of the self just as Watson suggested. The balance sheet, he argued, showed your strengths and your weaknesses so that you could work on them. At its best, psychological testing can do that.

In chapter 9 you will find a complex form which is your own Balance Sheet of the Self. It includes the following headings:

- Intelligence
- Personality
- Attitude/Ambition
- Creativity
- Social skills
- Individual interests
- Secret failings.

The balance sheet on pp. 135–8 has been designed so that you can assess yourself as you are *now* and then compare yourself after you have made some effort to get your act together. In all the following chapters, I encourage you to list your strengths and weaknesses. Truthful self-observation is a key part of filling in this balance sheet.

As no one prepares us to take psychological tests, it is easy to get over-anxious and to be dogged by the feelings of tension and inadequacy exams evoke – of frantic swotting to catch up with what you didn't learn in time, of fear your mind will go blank and of the feeling you didn't do justice to yourself.

The best way to deal with such anxieties is to confront and examine them. In a book on psychological tests, the obvious way to do this is through a specially designed test.

Don't get anxious. This test is really here to help you – and there are no right or wrong answers. The answers will give you information for your balance sheet and suggest to you skills you need to work on.

The testing test

1. Think of the times when you had to take examinations. Circle the adjectives that best describe your feelings then (you can circle more than one answer):
   a. excited
   b. scared
   c. anxious you wouldn't do justice to yourself

d   eager to get it over with
e   surprised you enjoyed it
f   felt that the whole process was unfair.

2. Do you think that the results you got in examinations reflected:
   a   how clever you were?
   b   how much work you put in?
   c   had no relationship to your ability?
   d   just showed you froze?

3. When you write or apply online for a job, do you expect:
   a   that they will not reply at all?
   b   that they will leap at the chance to employ you?
   c   that you will get a polite rejection?
   d   that you will get an interview and mess it up?

4. When you are unsure of yourself do you:
   a   hide it well from others?
   b   try to understand just what is making you nervous?
   c   you are never unsure!
   d   talk fast?

5. Which of the following describe best the way you feel about how you present yourself:
   a   very confident?
   b   fairly confident?
   c   average confidence?
   d   unconfident?
   e   total lack of confidence?

6. To do your best in any kind of interview situation, do you:
   a   just take it as it comes? I'm more relaxed that way.
   b   prepare very thoroughly by finding out as much as you can about the company?
   c   think it's all a question of fate?
   d   do a little preparation but not too much?

7. Which of the following make you feel good in a stressful work situation:
   a   being smartly dressed?

    b being well briefed?
    c a good horoscope that day?
    d very rarely do I feel good.

8. In your opinion, do you think that successful people are:
    a lucky?
    b work hard for their breaks?
    c happen to have been born with a silver spoon in their mouths?
    d are just more clever and dynamic than the rest of us?

9. The most important thing about getting a job is:
    a having the right connections.
    b having good references.
    c having a good track record.

10. Which of the following situations do you think this picture depicts:

    a a man who is being told off for poor performance?
    b a man who is being praised?
    c you can't tell?
    d two men deciding they are going to make a stand against the ludicrous ideas of the production department?

11. You take an interview and you do not get the job you had hoped for. Do you think that this is because
    a there were better candidates?

b the interviewer didn't like you?

c you weren't at your best and didn't make a proper pitch which displayed your abilities?

d bad luck?

e the job wasn't right for you?

12. Before making an application for a job, do you

  a discuss it with your partner?

  b discuss it with all your friends?

  c tell no one?

13. When you feel anxious, do you worry

  a that you are very twitchy?

  b that you are sweating?

  c that you will not know what to say?

  d this is not a concern?

  e that you talk too fast?

14. As soon as you walk through the door of a new company, do you

  a try to assess what it is like?

  b know whether it's the right place for you?

  c feel gloomy? Everyone here seems much smarter.

The so-called answers are given on p. 130. Remember this is not a test where you can score a high of 18 out of 20 or a low of 3 out of 20. The questions are designed to help you focus on how you approach the whole recruitment process – and what you can do to make it easier for yourself.

Among other things, the questions try to tease out the level of anxiety you are likely to feel when looking for a job and how you cope with this. Anxiety is the most acute problem people come up against in the recruitment process.

The Yerkes Dodson Law

There is a law in psychology called the Yerkes Dodson Law. This states that you are likely to do best in any task when you are moderately aroused but not too anxious. If you are not aroused at all, you won't care about your performance. If you are too aroused, you are likely to make careless mistakes or to freeze depending, very crudely, on whether you are extrovert or an introvert. Extroverts become careless; introverts freeze.

The desire to succeed can sometimes make us too keen. Good interviewers often notice this and try to put candidates at their ease. But it is much better if you know your own weaknesses and take steps to deal with them.

What to do if you are anxious

Be well prepared. For most people, anxiety is greater when they are dealing with the unknown and when they feel unprepared.

If you are at all worried, it is worth writing out a *check list* the night before you are going to see the company. Many of the points are obvious but when you are anxious, you can very easily forget to do the obvious. I have, in my time, turned up at the wrong place, hours too early or far too late and without the right equipment. No one should be too proud to devote a few moments to planning.

Planning

Make sure you know where you are going. Some companies operate from a number of addresses. Check just where you are expected to turn up. Work out how you are going to get there.

Leave in plenty of time. If you are using public transport, allow enough time in case there are hold-ups. If you are driving, allow enough time for bad traffic conditions.

Take a pencil and at least two biros. You may not need them. Everything may be done on computers, but better safe than sorry. The last thing you want to do is to have to ask to borrow writing materials. If you turn up without anything to write with, it looks as if you haven't bothered to think about what may be required of you.

Do some research on the company you are applying to. Make sure you know the kind of job that you are going for.

Be psyched up to have tests thrown at you. Work out what to say in response to the question 'Why do you want this job?' You may be asked that in an interview and/or in a test. Many tests now include open-ended questions.

Checklist

> Where am I going?
>
> How am I getting there?
>
> When should I leave?
>
> What does the company do?
>
> Pencils, biros, other gear.
>
> Why do I want the job?

Anxiety is not the problem for some of us. There are individuals who are more likely to ruin their chances by being over-confident or assuming that the job is theirs for the taking.

Most tests demand precision. Give yourself enough time to check what you have written. Highly extrovert people – who usually sell themselves well at interviews because they like talking and can exude charm – may find that tests bring out their careless side. If you are an extrovert, double your determination to check your answers.

Rehearsal

One problem with the Yerkes Dodson Law is that it was devised by looking at how people reacted in laboratory experiments. In such studies, subjects are asked to perform artificial tasks: to spot how many times a green light flashes on a screen or to go through the alphabet backwards. Going for a job is not an artificial process like this. Often people care desperately about whether they succeed or fail. The Yerkes Dodson Law does not quite apply so we need to look at different kinds of research to find strategies for coping.

The best answers come from sports psychology. Sportsmen and women care a great deal about how they perform – and get very anxious about it. Sports psychologists have found that athletes, basketball players, ice hockey teams and tennis players can handle high anxiety in competitive situations as long as they prepare for it well. The first step is to admit that they get anxious. Initially, many athletes resist admitting it.

Once you can say to yourself that you are anxious, you can rehearse ways of coping. Psychologists are now counselling top-class athletes on how to make positive use of their anxiety. A key strategy is known as 'mental rehearsal'.

Athletes imagine in great detail the event they are going to compete in. They imagine entering the stadium; getting changed; going out to the field of play; the various phases of the game.

Many athletes spend training sessions on visual imagery. They follow themselves going through the whole of the competition from arriving at the stadium to collecting their prizes. The British hurdler, David Hemery, who won the 400 metres hurdles in the 1968 Olympics, told a British Psychological Society conference he was sure this imagery had helped him win. He had even imagined standing on the podium and getting his medal!

There is no reason why you should not go through a comparable process in preparing yourself for interviews and being tested.

The first step is to relax. If you find it hard to relax, lie down on your bed or on a sofa, breathe deeply and clear your mind of all thoughts before you start imagining. One of the things this book offers is enough information for you to base your imaginings on. Call this 'Zen and the Art of Getting the Job You Want'.

When you feel relaxed, you should start the process of rehearsal and imagery.

SOME IMAGERY RULES

- Be specific in the mental images you conjure up.
- Rehearsal means much more than nice fantasies about what getting the job would be like. You should picture yourself overcoming problems you will face in the recruitment process.
- People going for a job here have a problem athletes don't have. Athletes know the stadium in which they are going to compete. They have a framework for their fantasies. You will probably not know the precise setting for taking the test

or being interviewed. Some people don't find it easy to visualize. Here is what you should do if that is hard.

EXERCISE

- Close your eyes.

- Think of a comparable setting in which you were tested or you went for a job interview before – preferably a setting in which you coped well.

- Actively imagine the questions you will ask if you find yourself confronted by a test you do not understand.

- Work on knowing what your weaknesses are and particularly on what makes you specially anxious.

- Actively imagine doing a test. There is enough practice material in this book to allow you to devise specific images of that. Let me sketch in some very basic cues which should help get your imagery going. One way to do this is to build up a sequence:
  – leaving home
  – the outside of the company building
  – arriving at reception
  – the interview room
  – the Personnel Officer, now often the Human Resource executive
  – the test
  – the interview questions
  – the answers you have prepared to open questions
  – asking for feedback
  – waiting for the result.

- Actively imagine asking for the results. All professional test organizations recommend that people who give tests should de-brief the individuals who take them. Key points of feedback you should ask for are:

  > What was the test trying to show?
  > Are they going to tell you how you did?
  > What part is it likely to play in their decisions? Don't be pushy about this but you have a right to know.

• Actively imagine success. What is it like to get the job?

This mixture of active imagination and working on your weaknesses should boost your confidence and mean that you go into the whole process of being tested in a positive frame of mind.

The answers to the test in this chapter are to be found in chapter 9 on stress and techniques for dealing with it. As you work through the following chapters and the various sections of tests I have included, try to bear in mind the main message of this chapter. If you have the right attitude to tests, you should not be fearful. You can use them to show off your various talents. And competent testers should make that as easy as possible. They should want to know what you can do for their company, not scare you off. Unfortunately, many testers do not seem to realize that.

3. **Accuracy tests**

Books on testing generally start by looking at IQ tests. But a basic skill that intelligent people have is that they can recognize things and patterns more quickly than the less intelligent. So some testers have really got down to basics with simple tests of accuracy.

Simple tests of accuracy

Many jobs require accuracy – and we are all capable of making silly or careless mistakes. These tests require you to check spellings and numbers.

In the numerical section, for example, you will be asked:

Are 12789 and 12798 the same, or different?

Are 3077 and 3077 the same, or different?

Are 772164 and 771164 the same, or different?

Are 0.2674 and 0.2764 the same, or different?

It does not look like rocket science but it is less easy when you have, as is typical, 160 sets of numbers to check in six minutes. That means you have – how many seconds per judgment?

Accuracy tests also examine verbal accuracy. The simplest form is a list of words and names spelled in two different ways:

Is T. G. Smythe the same as, or different from, T. G. Smith?
Is Priti Ramakrishnan the same as, or different from, Priti Ramakrishvan?

Again, the real problem is that you will be working against the clock.

There are variations on the test, as follows. Candidates may be asked:

In the following sentence, which word is spelled wrongly?

I wandered lonely as a clud among a sea of daffodils.

Curiously, the task becomes easier if there is more than one error in a text:

I wandered lonely as a clud among a see of daffodils.

TIPS

Prepare for this test by focusing. Give yourself 30 seconds before you are timed so that you can approach the six minutes in a calm way. If you feel sure you are right about a choice, make it instantly. Discipline yourself to stop after every 40 choices. In theory, you should be able to recognize whether a set of numbers are the same or different in 1.5 seconds.

So your timetable should look like this:

First 40 choices, each taking 1.5 seconds	60 seconds
Re-check, 0.5 secs each	20 seconds

So each batch of 40 choices should take 80 seconds, which means you should get to the end of the 160 in 320 seconds.
How many minutes is 320 seconds?
Five minutes and 20 seconds.
If you follow my advice, you will get to the end with 40 seconds to spare, so you can look back at any of the choices you have doubts about.

It is now time to look at the father and mother of psychometric tests, the IQ test.

4. **Intelligence tests**

Anthony is very bright. He is 17 and has got eight GCSEs with good grades. Yet Anthony finds it hard to fix a leaking tap. It is not just that he is clumsy but he does not seem able to visualize how to repair a leaking tap. He cannot break the problem down into manageable chunks.

Jenny is the opposite, shy and not very talkative. All her teachers thought she was quite dim. Yet practical tasks are no ordeal for her. Jenny is good with her hands and also quick at picking up anything musical. Maths and English scare her so people tend to think she is stupid. In fact, she is nothing of the kind.

You could describe both these characters more technically. Anthony could be said to have 'high verbal and mathematical intelligence but a low performance IQ', while Jenny has 'good performance and musical intelligence but scores poorly on verbal and numerical IQ'.

Many of us are good at some things and bad at others. The *Evening Standard* once asked three successful individuals to build some self-assembly furniture. None did it easily or quickly: the *Standard*'s art critic ended up, embarrassed, with bits of his wardrobe-to-be in disarray at his feet.

Psychologists have been arguing for a long time about whether intelligence is a general ability or whether it is a mosaic of distinct and specific skills. For nearly fifty years, most psychologists have argued that there is a general factor of intelligence which underlies how well we do everything. To be able to improve your performance, it is best to think of your intelligence as specific skills (see Figures 1, 2 and 3).

EXERCISE
An extension of the Balance Sheet of the Self is to list your particular strengths and weaknesses. With IQ, you can break these down into:

Potential strengths:

- Speed of dealing with problems
- Good with words
- Good visual grasp
- Good with numbers
- Sees fast how to fix things
- Persistent
- Good at seeing different ways to solve a problem

Weaknesses:

- Scared of maths
- Confused by visual puzzles
- Give up easily when you can't see the answer
- Feel insecure about intelligence

The lists aren't exclusive. The point of drawing them up is to get you to think about which aspects of your intelligence need practice and working on.

Figures 1, 2 and 3 show three ways of imagining the relationship between different kinds of intelligence. The fact that there are three ways points up how controversial IQ remains.

Yet the kind of test you are most likely to face is some variant of an IQ test. Since we all like to think of ourselves as intelligent, facing an IQ test can make us nervous. What if the results prove my ultimate aim in life should be nothing more than washing dishes in the El Greaso Transport Cafe?

By the time you have read this chapter, I hope you will be a bit less anxious about the outcome.

The history of IQ

The brilliant and eccentric Victorian scientist Francis Galton was one of the first to devise intelligence tests. Galton's tests included – rather prophetically – tests of how quickly people reacted to various stimuli like flashing dots. Galton believed there was an underlying general 'intelligence'. How well you did equations, could understand art and managed to cook, all

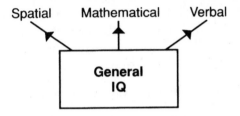

Figure 1. General IQ feeds each ability

Spatial   < >   Verbal   < >   Mathematical

Figure 2. Abilities connected, but loosely

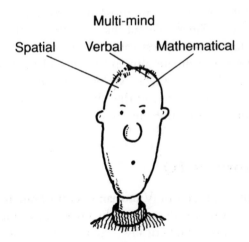

Figure 3. No links between abilities

reflected your general intelligence.

Galton's research had a hidden agenda. He believed in eugenics and wanted to encourage clever people to marry each other. The lower, dumber orders should be forbidden to breed.

Galton's eugenic mania was the first of many controversies around IQ. For the past 40 years, many left-wing psychologists have argued IQ tests discriminate against black people and working-class children. Many questions are framed by middle-class white people for middle-class white people, so the tests don't really test pure intelligence or reasoning. The results just show how well you have been educated and the social class to which you belong.

Defenders of IQ tests have tried to eliminate such 'contaminated' items and to devise 'culture-free' questions which are as easy – or as hard – for a Manhattan smart alec, an Eskimo or a poor Indian. How successful such attempts are remains controversial.

Ironically, the psychologists who worked on intelligence testing after Galton had liberal social motives. Breeding a race of 'super-brains' was the last thing on their mind.

In 1904, Theodore Simon and Alfred Binet were commissioned by the Parisian authorities to find out how to help children who were not doing well in normal school. Simon and Binet had to establish what it was normal for children of different ages to be able to learn. They had to define normal achievement at any age from birth to the age of 16 and hit on the notion of the intelligence quotient.

They worked out, for example, that it was normal for a child aged six to distinguish between morning and afternoon; to copy the picture of a diamond; to count 13 pennies and to distinguish between pictures of ugly and pretty faces.

By the age of eight, the normal child should be able to compare two objects from memory; to count from 0 to 20; to say what had been left out from a picture he or she had just seen; to give the day and the date; and to repeat back a list of five digits.

IQ expressed the relationship between what was normal for the child to achieve at a particular age and what any individual child actually achieved. The development of IQ tests became statistically complex but the basic idea was the same.

Individual score	7
Average score for that age	5
Then the IQ is	140 (as 7 divided by 5 = 1.4)

There are many different kinds of IQ test but nearly all of them derive from two very well established ones. One is called the Stanford Binet Test which used a lot of Binet's work; the other is the Wechsler test, first created in the 1930s. Both have been tested and re-tested over nearly 80 years. They are the most studied – and reliable – of psychological tests.

People easily get obsessed with IQ. Newspapers love child prodigies who dazzle us with amazing IQ scores. In fact, important though IQ is, it does not by itself guarantee success. Nor does having just an average IQ mean that you are destined to fail.

For most high-powered jobs you need only have an IQ of above 118. To get a first class honours degree you need an IQ of 120, above average but not vastly so. Many people with first class degrees – and many successful people – would not have a hope of being admitted into Mensa.

We think of the average IQ as 100. It is no longer that, however. The average IQ for white Caucasians is now about 106, and for Asians it is higher and has been reckoned as about 109.

You would think that people would be pleased we were getting brighter. But no. IQ has always been a controversial subject, with those whose political views are on the right sometimes thinking there is a conspiracy against tests. According to the American Stephen Sailer in 2002, 'This century's most talked-about – but least written-about – book of underground social science has been *IQ and the Wealth of Nations*, by Richard Lynn and Tatu Vanhanen.'

What has made this book such dynamite? The authors compared 184 studies of IQ for 81 countries. The results were dramatic. 'Average IQ and per capita Gross Domestic Product [GDP] correlated – at the kind of high level that social scientists mostly only dream of finding,' Sailer said.

In other words, the higher the IQ score of a country, the

more economically successful it is. But this has to be kept secret.

Sailer complained that the book got no attention at all in the USA, home of the politically correct. But worse, in Finland the police arrested one of the authors, Vanhanen. Vanhanen is not actually a dangerous criminal but an emeritus professor of political science at two different Finnish universities. His son also happened to be Finland's prime minister when the book was published.

Said prime minister had to apologize for his father's awfully politically incorrect claim that the more intelligent a country is, the wealthier it is, and in the end Vanhanen was not jailed (UPI, Finland, 12 August 2004).

Sailer argues that the data in the book makes it very obvious that tests show consistent results and predict success. And who are the most consistent of all? Probably the Swiss, whose minds tick as consistently as their watches. Three studies across 30 years showed they scored average IQs of 101, 99 and 102. Some countries were more wayward. The Poles and the Portuguese were all over the place. But overall, the IQ scores were consistent, and the higher the IQ score, the greater the wealth of that country. African countries did not score well.

The Far East, on the other hand, was brilliant. 'Overall, the data when grouped into regions or races seems quite consistent. For example, among Northeast Asians (Koreans, Japanese, and Chinese), 24 of the 26 studies they uncovered reported scores between 100 and 110.'

The highest-scoring country was Hong Kong. Five studies, three with sample sizes of 4,500 or more, gave average adjusted scores of 103, 110, 109, 107 and 107.

But why are Asians brainier? Is it their genes? Is it their diet? Does sushi make you smarter? Fans of P. G. Wodehouse will remember that his amazingly intelligent butler Jeeves always ate fish (though if it was raw, we were never told). Fish was good for the brain, Wodehouse believed. This is not codswallop, as it were. Much research suggests the fatty oils in fish are excellent brain food. It was his diet which gave Jeeves the intellectual edge over those who preferred steak and kidney pie!

The subject of the fairness of tests is an important one, to which we will return with Muhammad Ali.

Muhammad Ali versus Jeeves – now there's a fight I'd have liked to see!

Full intelligence test

A full intelligence test is long and complicated. Very few prospective employers are likely to ask you to fill one in. They are much more likely to use shortened – and sometimes coarsened – versions of the tests.

Though most psychologists believe that there is a general factor of intelligence, intelligence tests are divided up into questions that probe a number of specific abilities. The most important are:

- verbal ability
- numerical ability
- spatial ability
- practical ability.

For lower-level jobs, intelligence tests are often the main part of the process. Capita Ras, the large British recruitment agency, were recently involved in hiring 150 people to a call centre. 'We looked at verbal and numerical reasoning and we also did a test for data awareness. The staff needed to sound as if they had a head on their shoulders,' Rosemary Moore of Capita told me.

The main additional skill Capita wanted to test was one that companies don't necessarily want to advertise. The call centre inevitably had to handle complaints. 'Staff would be dealing with a lot of angry customers who had a lot of complaints.' Capita Ras don't blab about who they recruit for, but intuition – a quality psychometric tests don't pick up well – made me make the outrageous guess that their client was a gas company.

'My lips are sealed,' said Ms Moore, who burst out laughing. For their Anonymous Gas client, Capita devised a cunning second test. Candidates had to reply to a letter from an angry consumer, Outraged of Tunbridge Wells, the British equivalent of Outraged of Westport, Connecticut.

Exercises like the letter help agencies to present assessment as a 'holistic process'. 'We would never suggest that a job be given solely on psychometric testing,' Rosemary Moore told me. 'In fact we recently refused a job where all a client wanted us to do was to test verbal and numerical competency.'

But the letter exercise has its own perils. Imagine you were faced with the problem. Should you write a letter to Outraged of Tunbridge Wells which apologized and admitted the gas company was at fault or a letter which vigorously defended the gas company? One manager might want a complaints person who was soft with consumers; another manager would prefer one who was hard.

Despite thousands of articles which point to their problems, intelligence tests remain the most widely used tests – and the ones recruiters usually place most faith in. There's even evidence that the interviews candidates face if they get through the tests are affected by testing. 'It's fair comment to say that the tests suggest questions you have to ask,' said psychologist Glen Fox. Interviewers like to say the test answers help them 'probe the competencies'.

This puts more pressure on those who take tests. They not only have to try to do them well but they also have to try to remember what kind of answers they gave, in order to be well prepared for interviews.

There is one other important point. Psychologists distinguish between two kinds of thinking – *convergent* thinking and *divergent* thinking. Convergent thinking focuses on solving puzzles to which there is only one correct answer. You can either fill in the missing digit in the sequence 2, 4, 6, . . . , 10 correctly or not.

Many questions however do not have a right or wrong answer. If a group of executives has to work out the best sales strategy for a new cosmetic brand, or if a group of railway engineers has to work out the most efficient scheduling for repairing the signalling between Brighton and Victoria, there are many options. Some will be better, some worse, but no one option is the only right one. Such questions require divergent thinking. Intelligence tests only really deal with convergent – right or wrong – thinking and usually rely just on multiple choice questions where you have to pick the correct answer. It is important to get a sense of the variety of questions that crop up in IQ tests.

Creating concepts

Pioneers of IQ emphasized that intelligence required:

   i.   the ability to see associations between ideas;
  ii.   the ability to work out similarities and differences;
 iii.   the ability to see logical relationships.

The following kinds of questions always occur in tests:

In what ways are cows and horses alike?
In what ways are rivers and roads the same?

A variant asks people to find out which is the odd one out in the following four: a dog, a cow, a pig, a flower.
   Such questions can be put in words or visually.

One carrot: four carrots
One pencil: . . .

All these questions ask you to find the link between different objects that distinguishes them from other objects.
   The emphasis on logic came because the pioneers of IQ wanted to get at the basic atoms of thinking – logical relations. A number of questions aim to see if you can work through the steps of a logical problem:

If A is larger than B, and B is larger than C, A has to be larger than C.

Questions do not just depend on size. Take the following:

All men are mortal
Aristotle is a man
Therefore Aristotle is . . .

Success is also a question of speed. Intelligence testing has always involved an element of doing it against the clock. Descriptions we use to contrast bright, and less bright, individuals include being 'quick' or 'quick on the uptake', and being 'slow'. Till recently, there wasn't much of a theory behind such talk. In the last few years, there has been some interesting evidence that suggests that one surprisingly useful test of IQ can be very simple.

- Flash coloured dots and tell subjects to press when they see the RED dot.
- Show subjects a series of lines and get them to press a buzzer as soon as they see one that has a cross with a circle on top.

Some psychologists now claim that reaction time, in a situation where the subject has to choose between two stimuli, is the purest test of intelligence. Others dispute that hotly, saying the experiments look elegant but actually leave out all the complexities of intelligence. So far, few industries have paid much attention to this new theory. Speed isn't everything.

Though few employers will give a full-scale Wechsler Adult Intelligence Scale, any competent test will look at at least four different aspects of intelligence – verbal ability scales, numerical ability, spatial ability and performance ability.

Verbal ability

The way someone speaks seems to reveal much about their intelligence. In a very class-conscious society like Britain, people with 'posh' accents are usually thought of as more intelligent than people with 'rough' working-class accents. But accents aren't brains.

In analysing IQ tests the trick is to see what else, apart from pure reasoning, they are testing. Many verbal questions aim to test whether people understand the relationships behind the words. Sometimes that is less easy than it looks. Some questions require no hidden knowledge.

A typical easy question like the one below assumes only the very basic knowledge of colours that a two-year-old child will normally have:

Black is to white as
Small is to . . .
Choose from brown, large, vicious, tiny.

What the test is looking for is an opposite like *large*. But sometimes the relationship is less black and white. The following question is a little less easy, though again it doesn't assume much knowledge:

Bee is to sting as

Dog is to . . .

Choose from eat, paw, cat, hound, bite.

The answer is *bite* since that is how dogs attack.

Verbal questions, however, often demand sophisticated knowledge of vocabulary and even general knowledge. Pure reasoning skill is just part of what you need. Take even a simple question. Which of the following words means the same as mend in 'mend the tyre' – patch, clean, change, fill? How easy is that for a non car owner? The answer is *patch*.

A second example. What is, for example, another word for *tome* – book, mansion, grave, tomb? Surely that question, the answer to which is *book*, is easier for middle-class bookworms who will have heard people talk of books, volumes, folios and not been foxed by them. Then, there are the 'opposites' questions.

ADAMANT is the opposite of:

dull, unlike Adam, stubborn, yielding.

Adamant is a very rarely used word indeed. Literary types might be familiar with it. Others perhaps less so. The answer is *yielding*.

Some verbal questions look more 'pure' like:

Do you know . . . this train goes to Oxford?

Choose from: what, although, after, which, whether.

But even here what is being tested is not so much intelligence as grammatical knowledge of what makes a correct sentence.

Other questions look very much like questions of pure logic, such as:

Only fish have fins, therefore which of the following statements is true:

    i. fish use their fins to propel themselves through the water

    ii. birds don't have fins

    iii. all fins are like legs on mammals.

This question requires more than logical skill. The more general knowledge you have, especially some basic idea of fish anatomy, the easier it is to get right. If you have no idea of how fish swim, the question may defeat you. The answer is that all the statements are true.

Most people are likely to have some clue about how fish swim but you have to have some specialist knowledge to be able to make sense of the following:

> Physicist is to Botanist as Atom is to . . .
> butterflies, social problems, plant, stars, Botany Bay.

You need to know that physicists study atoms to have a hope of giving the correct answer, which is *plant*.

Below are some sample IQ test questions. It might be a useful exercise not just to answer them but to jot down what verbal knowledge they demand other than pure reasoning.

It is obviously easier to answer such questions if you are well educated, have a good vocabulary and a knowledge of grammar.

Being able to answer such questions is also a matter of culture. Someone who lived in a culture where science did not exist would have no clue about the difference between physicists and botanists. They just would not be able to 'compute' that question.

The verbal IQ scales of both the Stanford Binet and the Wechsler do correlate very well with academic performance. According to Paul Kline, who was one of Britain's leading psychological test experts, the correlation is something of the order of 0.5. Statistically, this is impressive.

IQ test questions

Verbal ability

1. *Komala Monoharam* means 'A lovely lotus' in Sanskrit. 'The lotus is in the pond' is, in Sanskrit, *Tadage Vartati Komala.*
   What is the Sanskrit for lotus?
   What is the Sanskrit for lovely?

2. Find a word that can go into the bracket and make a word with all these:
   SC (. . .) end
   T (. . .)
   B (. . .)
   SP (. . .)

3. Find a word that can go into the bracket. It must have at least four letters
   F (. . . .)
   C (. . . .)
   (. . . .) ING
   SP (. . . .)

4. Fill in the word in the bracket
   SH (. . .) ER
   so that you get two words

5. Fill in the word in the bracket so that each word makes sense ROUND (. . . . .) TURN

6. Fee (tip) end
   Dance (   ) sphere
   What is the missing word?

7. How many sports in LOOP? And what are they? *pool*
   polo

8. If tomorrow were Monday, yesterday would be Sunday. Is this true, false, can't tell? *No*

Some IQ tests include general knowledge questions which also require some verbal acrobatics. Each of the following is scrambled:

9. Which of the following is not a famous poet?
   Obynr, Skate, Dorswrthow, Omesal, Onlimt.

10. Which of the following is not a famous composer?
    Drive, Zomrat, Pincho, Hoetvebne, Rubste.

11. Which of the following is not a famous artist?
    Laid, Egrife, Gritmeta, Sitmase, Ospicas.

(For the answers to these questions, see p. 68.)

TIPS

The verbal sections of an IQ test are likely to feel most familiar to readers, especially to the many millions who doodle at puzzles and do Quick Crosswords in newspapers. A good way to practise is to do such puzzles because they often demand the same trains of thought as IQ tests do.

Tip one. *If the test is long, use your watch so that you keep track of how much time you have left. IQ tests are not like essay examinations where two really good essays may get you through if you run out of time before you write the third.*

Tip two. *Answers may seem obvious but check the questions. Verbal questions can be confusing. Often people confuse whether they are being asked to give the word that means the same as or the word that means the opposite of a particular word.*

Tip three. *Remember the limitations of such verbal testing. If you are interviewed and they discuss how you did, you should know the following:*

- The questions in verbal IQ tests do not measure how you use language or, especially, how creative your use of language might be. Someone who uses language originally – whether they happen to be a poet or someone who can put together a good pitch for a new product – might not do particularly well on the verbal scales.
- The questions are nearly always put in basically 'received' posh language with conventional spelling.

Numerical ability

The numerical parts of intelligence tests are most like exams. Questions look at how you can deal with addition, subtraction, multiplication and division. But, here too, the purpose is to get at basic numerical reasoning skills – not learned mathematical ability.

The most basic item used to test numerical ability is known as Digit Span. People are read a number of digits and just asked to repeat them back, like the sequence 9, 4, 7, 1, 8. There is a harder version of this test. People are read a stream of usually seven digits. They are then asked to repeat them backwards. This test is as much a test of memory as of numerical ability though scores on it correlate fairly well with intelligence, and especially well with intelligence as one ages.

A favourite question is that of a sequence of numbers with a missing digit. Many of these puzzles are fairly simple as in the following sequence:

2, 4, 6, ——, 10

The missing number is 8. But there are trickier sequences too:

2, ——, 8, ——, 128

Here the $2 \times 4 = 8$. The next number is $8 \times 16 = 128$. The next number has to be 128×256. The sequence is the answer of the last sum multiplied by its double. No specialist mathematical knowledge is needed. Compare:

3, ——, 7, ——, 11, ——, X

The blanks are easy to fill but X could either be the next number plus 4 (15) or the next prime number which is 17. Knowing prime numbers requires technical knowledge.

Numerical questions are not always mathematical:

(a) 14 days (b) a fortnight
Is the length of time in (a) longer than (b), shorter than (b), or the same period?

Number questions can also be set in words:

A car does half a trip at 30 miles an hour but the rest of the drive is on the motorway and it goes at 60 miles an hour. If the whole trip was 30 minutes long, how far has the car gone?

Companies often adapt this style of question to the needs of their particular industry, making prospective candidates juggle sums they might pay for stamps, carpets or tyres.

Studies of school children show that mathematics creates probably more anxiety than any other subject. Some people feel they just cannot handle numbers. Many adults have the same problem and, worse, they feel ashamed of it which is likely to make them especially anxious as they take the test.

Examples of mathematical questions

TIP

Do not get intimidated by the numbers.

NUMERICAL QUESTIONS

1. Margaret is taller than Kathy, Kathy is taller than Joan, who is the tallest?

2. In a class there are 30 children: 20 boys and 10 girls. Half the class play cricket and half the class play hockey. Do any boys play hockey?

3. Fill in either plus or minus signs in the following sequences:
   3 2 3 = 8
   11 6 8 4 = 9

4. Fill in the asterisks in the following:
   3764, 4376, 6437, ★★★★

5. What are the missing numbers in the circle?

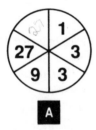

A   B

6. What are the next two numbers in this series?
   7, 11, 9, 14, 12, 18, . . . , . . .

7. What is the odd number out in this sequence?
   144, 169, 625, 224, 256

8. What is the missing number?
   14, 28, 49
   16, 32, 64
   8, 16, XX

9. Fill in the missing fractions:

$$\frac{16}{18} \quad \frac{14}{21} \quad \frac{17}{19} \quad \frac{13}{22} \quad —$$

(For the answers to these questions, see p. 68.)

HARDER QUESTIONS

For adults, there are no levels of IQ test. There is no Ordinary IQ test followed by the Advanced IQ test followed by the IQ test that only Einstein could have passed. IQ tests should not include questions like the Enigma brain-teasers which appear in the *New Scientist*. These are real logical puzzles which, like some very complex crossword puzzles, demand not just a high level of IQ but also a peculiar gift for solving that kind of problem. IQ questions are less idiosyncratic.

What will make some parts of an IQ test easier and some harder is not just the questions but your particular strengths and weaknesses. That is why it is so important to keep building up your balance sheet of the self.

TIPS

Tip one. *Many number questions involve sequences. Try first to see if there is any obvious pattern in the differences between numbers. Do they all go up by 2 or by 2×2 or does the first go up by 4 (2×2), and the next by 9 (3×3)? That would suggest the next one should go up by 16 (4×4). In question 9 the numbers on top go up by 1 and + and − signs alternate −2, +3, −4 so that the next number should be +5. The sequence in the bottom is +3, −2, +3 so it should be −2. The answer is $\frac{18}{20}$.*

Tip two. *Practice will help make you less anxious about this which is why I have set out a page of such problems. Again it is worth doing the easy mathematical puzzles in puzzle magazines just to get used to this kind of problem solving.*

The Sudoku craze and its uses

One of the things that has changed in the last few years is the craze for Sudoku. Every newspaper carries examples of the game. Each square is made up of nine numbers, and you can't repeat any number in any horizontal or vertical line. No test organization uses Sudoku, to my knowledge, but they are very good games for practising your number skills. I offer a very simple puzzle for any readers who are not familiar with it. But I urge you to do at least one such game or puzzle daily. They are fun and they are very good for anyone who worries about their skills with numbers. (For the solution, see p. 151.)

	2	7	9			3		
		3						
						4		8
1	6	9	8	2				
		4	1	3		2		
								5
3			4	8	6			
			3				6	
9								

Spatial ability

The pioneers of IQ worked at a time when psychologists were fascinated by how the brain processes visual patterns. It was natural to include visual questions and this has paid off because there are clearly people who may not be good with words or numbers but who are smart with space.

Many good chess players say that when they see a chess board, they don't see just the pieces but, also, spatial and power relationships. They see how the pawn in the middle of the board can become a major player. The pieces are seen as a pattern – both as they are now, and as they could be. Most of us are not good chess players but our brains try to make patterns out of the most confusing material.

Typically, questions give a number of patterns or signs and ask you to fill in either the missing box or the next square. A favourite test of spatial intelligence is the picture completion test where for example you get a house with windows and a path but no door. The spatially astute will spot the need to add the door.

Two examples

In doing spatial questions, one important clue is to break down the pattern. For example, if you are presented with a question like 1, look at the squares, noses, eyes and mouth. Each varies from picture to picture.

1.

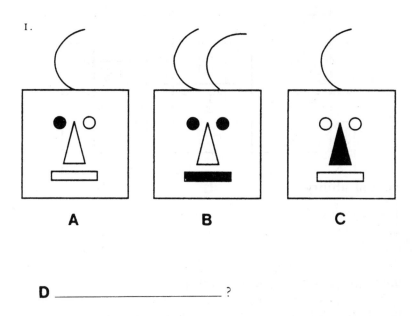

A   **B**   **C**

D _____ ?

Often spatial questions rotate figures, so that you are asked to say that if A is to B then which of 6 figures is in the same relation to C. Here you need again to select out each chunk of the pattern for analysis.

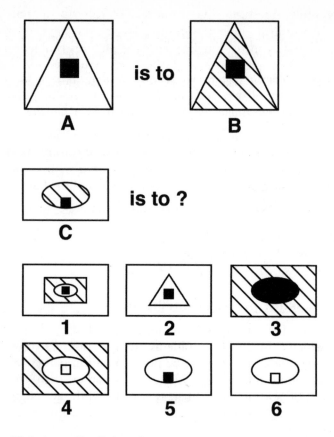

2. If A is to B, C is to?

(For the answers to these questions, see p. 68.)

No culture? Much better

A number of psychologists have experimented with essentially visual puzzles. Here vocabulary and general knowledge cannot matter. The reality is a little more complex. There is no doubt that people who live in societies where squares, circles and rectangles are regularly seen will be more at ease with such puzzles.

When you have studied the puzzles, which is useful practice, imagine how hard they would be for someone who was not used to seeing abstract patterns.

TIPS

Tip one. *A fresh point of view can help if you are stuck on a visual puzzle. Look away or close your eyes and then look again.*

Tip two. *Draw the figures out yourself, rotating them as in question 2 above. If you build up the figure from scratch you are more likely to understand the elements and tricks it contains.*

Tip three. *If you still can't see what the puzzle is about don't get obsessed with it and forget to do the rest of the items. Move on.*

EXERCISE

Again, assess your own strengths and weaknesses, like:

- Prefer things in words.
- The puzzles look baffling.
- Not clear what are the key details.

Special skills: practical intelligence

There are IQ problems that appear to deal with practical intelligence. Usually the problems are very abstract, however, involving blocks that have to be put together in particular ways or assembling things from design kits rather than the real business of sorting out what is wrong with an engine or plumbing. Such mechanical tests tend to come under tests for special skills.

It is impossible, in a general book, to give an outline of the kinds of special skill tests that you might be given, since these will differ from job to job. What it is possible to do is to draw together some general guidelines on how to deal with IQ questions that are baffling or difficult:

- Make sure you understand what the question is looking for. Do they want a synonym, an opposite word, an anagram or a number sequence?
- If you are really baffled, move on and then come back to this question. IQ tests are against the clock so you must be careful not to get bogged down. It isn't like some exams where one brilliant essay may compensate for two bad ones.
- Try to break down the problems, especially numerical and spatial ones, into chunks so that you can follow the logic.

Steps to the solution of number problems often involve looking at the relationships between all the numbers horizontally, all the numbers vertically and what the sums of the numbers are. You should try a number of alternative solutions. The same is true for verbal questions, like find a four-letter word that makes all the following words: G(. . . .) T(. . . .) (. . . .)Y REF(. . . .)

- Get into the habit of juggling with alternative solutions. That will also be useful in the Creativity section.

Rival ideas

Multi minds, frames of mind, and other mental mosaics

Three influential theories in the last 15 years have broken with the model of intelligence that IQ tests are based on. All of them dispute the importance of a general factor of intelligence. Rather, they suggest that what we take to be intelligence is a mosaic of different abilities. You may be very good at some and very bad at others. IQ tests fail because they try to arrive at one total score that reveals all your mental capacities. Your strengths and weaknesses may well be obscured in this total score.

Howard Gardner, a psychologist at Harvard, has claimed most recently in *Multiple Intelligences* (1994) that there are seven different kinds of intelligence. These are verbal, numerical, spatial, artistic, movement, musical and practical.

Robert Ornstein, a psychologist at Stanford University, has developed independently rather similar ideas. Ornstein argues that we have 'multi minds' – not just different intelligences – and that the brain has different compartments which compete with each other for control of the Executive. You have, for example, a verbal mind, an analytic mind, an artistic mind, a mathematical mind and so on.

A third psychologist, Robert Sternberg, has argued that tests of intelligence ought to include more emphasis on social intelligence because intelligence is exercised often between people. It is not just a question of how you understand a puzzle like Raven's Matrices, but how you use your ability in social situations to persuade people of your arguments, for example.

After the 1914–18 war, it took about 40 years for the IQ test to become widely used in industry. Things move more swiftly now and some tests already try to investigate what different kinds of intelligence a particular person shines at. For many employers, such new tests will be very useful because they will make it possible to pinpoint what employees are really good at – and what jobs you should never give them unless you want chaos to reign.

These new perspectives mean that IQ tests continue to raise some controversial questions (see p. 60).

In-tray exercises

Intelligence tests tend to be abstract. In-tray exercises are concrete. They can't claim to be scientifically validated but they are increasingly used especially for senior jobs once candidates have passed through the first round of recruitment.

Essentially, the idea is simple. Candidates are given a series of problems in their in-tray and have to jot quickly how they would solve them. In-tray exercises are tailored to particular industries. What you'd ask someone who was going for a job in a bank is utterly different to what you'd ask someone going for a job as a manager in a National Health Trust. In-tray exercises are supposed to be realistic. If they're well designed, the issues will come out of real life experiences in similar jobs. Don't try to pose as a magician. You can't solve a huge budget overspend by a simple formula, but what you can do is make sure you know why the budget is overspent, take action to prevent it getting worse, check that there are proper information procedures and so on. In-tray exercises should show that you have a good sense of what it is logical to do next.

Here are some examples of the dilemmas you might be asked to deal with if you were going for a management job in a health authority:

- You discover there's been an overspend of 14 per cent on the drugs budget and that most of it is in one part of your district.
- There are five letters of complaint about the amount of time

people have to wait when they come in for appointments to see the paediatric department. The consultant is a bully but something needs to be done.

- One of the local councillors has been pressing his GP to get a perfectly routine hernia operation reclassified as urgent. The GP is pressing for an immediate bed.
- Pharmaceutical companies offer to help fund a local research project. Your boss asks you to prepare a brief on the safeguards you need to see the authority isn't exploited.
- Patients from six years ago threaten to sue the authority because one of its surgeons didn't use what was the best procedure for heart by-pass operations.

One way of preparing for such in-tray exercises is to talk to colleagues and get a group to devise questions you 'play' with each other.

Key questions

- Are tests fair for everyone?
- Can you train to do better on them?
- Do they predict how well people will do in jobs?

Are tests fair?

This has been at the heart of political rows about IQ and other psychometric tests. Liberal psychologists argue that the tests discriminate against blacks, who score on average one standard deviation (about 12 IQ points) lower than whites. This does not mean that an individual black is likely to be less intelligent than an individual white but that, on average, a black population will be.

In 1995, the American Supreme Court voted narrowly to reverse affirmative action practices which had given blacks some protection.

And there clearly is a right-wing lobby that wants to prove that even famous and 'loved' black stars are really thick, as old stereotypes suggested.

In a controversial article on the website VDARE.com, called

'Solving the African IQ Conundrum: "Winning Personality" Masks Low Scores', Phil Rushton mused about why Africans did so badly on tests – and thus never made engineers or managers – while they had 'such bright, lively personalities'.

Instead of focusing on Nelson Mandela or Kofi Annan or even Robert Mugabe, who is no intellectual slouch, Rushton focused on Muhammad Ali. He examined what he called 'a wonderful Muhammad Ali–Howard Cosell exchange to show the black gift for coming up with subjectively delightfully unstandardized answers – a talent that objective standardized tests, by their very nature, can't measure':

> 'I'm gonna whoop him, Howard. You just watch!', Ali started.

> Cosell responded, 'You're feeling very truculent today, Muhammad.'

> Without batting an eye (or opening a dictionary), Ali uttered one of his trademark retorts, 'Truculent? If that's good, I'm it!'

The exchange makes it sound as if Ali had problems with his vocabulary, but, in fact, Ali was deft with words as well as with punches. Famously he said, 'Dance like a butterfly, sting like a bee.' But Rushton adds that Ali scored only 78 IQ points on the military's entrance exam. Ali always denied intentionally trying to score low.

So, Rushton claims, Ali was always basically stupid.

Rushton does not consider another explanation: Ali was hardly bothering with the test. He was not trying to do well, the way people usually do try when they take tests for job selection. And he may well have been taking the mickey at some points. The only nice thing Rushton says – and, to be fair, it is nice – is that Ali 'was intuitive, glib, richly gregarious, and intensely creative, like an artist'.

As we shall see in the chapter on tests of creativity, anyone who is highly creative will also tend to be highly intelligent. IQ is an important part of creativity.

Perhaps the most intriguing and consistent finding is that Asian children have the highest average IQ of any group. Studies that compare average IQ over the past 50 years suggest that average IQ is rising. It was 102 in 1950: now it is 107. No one is sure why Asian children should have a higher IQ. Some psychologists suggest that IQ is rising, like height, because standards of nutrition and hygiene in the developed world are rising. Pictorial culture-free tests discriminate less against non-whites but many psychologists still worry that they are not totally fair.

Does training help?

The conventional answer is No. You can't build up your IQ as you can your stamina. No study, however, has looked at the effect of doing newspaper puzzles on IQ. Psychologists tend to see such puzzles as tabloid trash. It seems likely that doing them will help – if only by making the type of puzzle familiar.

Do intelligence tests predict how you will do at anything else? Is it more than an academic game?

This research is controversial and not easy to interpret. The evidence strongly suggests that scores on the tests do predict academic performance well. Whether they predict success in jobs is more problematic. Everything depends on the demands of the job, and some of these may not be intellectual.

Banks when they recruit place a great deal of emphasis on basic number skills, for example, as does the Post Office. The Post Office has a Psychology Department and has done a great deal of research into aptitude testing of recruits and employees.

But good bank clerks and post office counter clerks need more than a good head for figures. A post office clerk who is always rude to customers and lectures old age pensioners on how generous the pensions they get are is not an asset. The numerate bank clerk may impress and, after some years, become a manager. But here number skills matter much less. What is important is the ability to assess risk and to make good lending recommendations to the bank's credit committee. Being numerate still matters, but it is no guarantee of success.

In other words, in the real world of industry, IQ matters but it is only part of the picture. That should not deter you from working on your strengths and weaknesses.

The Proving Paradox

IQ tests are, of all tests, the ones most like school exams. Many people will desperately want to do well and feel themselves tense up before they take them. It is worth repeating my advice on how to deal with tension.

- Relax. If you feel particularly tense, try to clear your mind of distracting thoughts before you start. Breathe deeply a few times.
- Be well prepared. You should by now have an idea of the kinds of questions you will be asked so that you need not be worried about nasty surprises being sprung on you.
- If you cannot do a question, don't worry about it. Move on. Time matters in almost all IQ tests.
- Make sure you read the questions properly – especially ones where you are asked to give a word that means the same as or opposite. These are very easy to mix up.

Inevitably, many of us experience conflicts about exams of any sort. The Proving Paradox is a description I have devised for something that people have observed for a long time. Many of us resent having to prove ourselves. Why should bosses or experts sit in judgement on us? That kind of resentment often makes people careless, cocky or just so fed up they don't really try. Don't sabotage yourself!

The hot test now

One increasingly popular test which is a kind of super-intelligence test is the Graduate Management Admission Test (GMAT).

It doesn't require straightforward answers to straightforward questions, but tests your ability to think critically. One feature is the Analytical Writing Assessment (AWA). The idea is simple. You are given two 30-minute writing tasks – 'Analysis of an Issue' and 'Analysis of an Argument'. In theory, say the test-builders, you do not need to have any detailed knowledge of the subject involved.

The idea, according to the test publishers, is that 'the Analysis of an Issue tests your ability to explore the complexities of an issue and to take a position that is informed by your understanding'. You are given about 300 words to read on a hot topic like climate change, and are then asked to analyse the subject and give your own point of view.

Don't worry about being right or wrong, they say. What the markers want to see is that you can look at a subject from many different angles and give examples drawn from your own experience or reading.

The publishers of the test do not allow other authors to reproduce the actual questions they use, so as an example I have devised one similar to the ones you may face.

Let's assume that the text you are given runs something like this:

> Every morning 200,000 commuters go through Waterloo Station on their way to work. There are still many complaints about the punctuality and cleanliness of trains. Many commuter groups protest that the railway companies are not investing enough in new rolling stock. The companies claim that the unions create problems and that there are high levels of absenteeism. The government threatens to revoke the licences of some of the railway companies. They have organized a series of public hearings where some of these issues are to be discussed.
>
> What issues do you expect to be raised at the public meeting?
>
> What are the reasons travellers complain?
>
> What is likely to be raised at the public meeting?

Of course, there is enough in the text above to allow you to write something, whether or not you have ever been on a train. But sheer common sense makes it obvious that the person who treks on the 8.14 to Waterloo every morning will have a more practical sense of the issues – as well as some useful experiences to bring his or her answers to life.

The GMAT is extremely highly regarded, but this particular aspect of it reminds me of the essays we used to have to do at school. In one way that's not bad, but detailed knowledge always helps in that kind of exercise.

Analysis of an Argument

For the Analysis of an Argument section, you will need to analyse and criticize the reasoning behind a given argument. Again, say the testers, you are not being asked to present your own views on the subject.

In the advice they give, they suggest that, in a good answer, you will consider the following when developing your essay:

- What assumptions underlie the thinking behind the argument?
- What alternative explanations or counterexamples might weaken the conclusion?
- What sort of evidence could help strengthen or refute the argument?

The test also has a quantitative section which measures the ability to reason quantitatively, solve quantitative problems and interpret graphic data. Two types of multiple-choice questions are used in the quantitative section of the GMAT test – problem-solving and data sufficiency.

Both types of question require knowledge of:

- arithmetic;
- elementary algebra;
- commonly known concepts of geometry.

Problem-solving questions

Problem-solving questions are designed to test:

- basic mathematical skills;
- understanding of elementary mathematical concepts;
- the ability to reason quantitatively and solve quantitative problems.

But perhaps the most complex questions are what they call:

Data-sufficiency questions

Data-sufficiency questions are designed to measure your ability to:

- analyse a quantitative problem;
- recognize which information is relevant;

- determine at what point there is sufficient information to solve a problem.

Let me give an example.

In the recent past it has become all too clear that the way we use fossil fuels such as coal and oil has a large impact on climate. Increased concentrations of greenhouse gases such as carbon dioxide and methane will lead to global warming. There has been research which suggests that icebergs are melting so fast in the Arctic that by 2050 there will be none left and the sea level will rise all over the globe. But other scientists remain more sceptical. They believe there will be increased precipitation at the poles, and they also point to the fact that the polar regions were once much warmer.

In the following questions, you have to say whether the paragraph above gives you enough information to decide whether the statements are true or false, or simply that you do not have enough information to make a judgement.

1. The depletion of the ozone layer will result in global warming.
2. Scientists are all agreed that our increased use of fossil fuels will eventually lead to a rise in sea levels.
3. The burning of fossil fuels leads to an increase in the concentration of carbon dioxide in the atmosphere.
4. If we do not have international agreements to reduce burning of fossil fuels, climate change will happen.

Question 1 is easy, as nothing in the text mentions the ozone layer. You don't have enough information.

Question 2 looks easy, but it isn't. The question asks whether all scientists believe burning more fossil fuels will lead to climate change. Most do, that is true.

But there are some sceptics. So the claim is false.

Question 3 is true, just given the first two sentences. The fact that some scientists are sceptical about the rise in sea level does not mean they don't agree with their non-sceptical colleagues on other questions. It would be false to say that burning fossil fuels leads to rises in sea level, but they all seem to agree that burning such fuels does increase the level of carbon dioxide.

Question 4 is false, because scientist don't all agree on the basic premise that burning more fossil fuels will lead to global warming. Precipitation might compensate.

Numerical questions

The GMAT test also has numerical questions like the following:

Mr Big works for a company which has an insurance scheme so that employees who are sick get:

- full pay for the first two months of sickness;
- half pay for months 3 to 6 they are sick;
- quarter pay for months 7 to 12.

How much does the scheme pay to William, who is off work for three months and whose normal salary is £30,000?

TIP

These are tricky questions. Take your time and consider alternatives. For the verbal questions, make out a little grid on which you can map the implications of the statements in the text. For the numerical questions, double-check your answers.

The Graduate Management Admission Test combines scores from different tests, and so does a simpler and newer test which has been tried out in Leeds.

The Decision Analysis Test

In the real world you often have to make sense of different kinds of information. One new test based on this is the Decision Analysis Test (DAT), which examines how you combine your abilities to solve problems, and how you use them to manage increasing amounts of information and deal with situations where you need to make a judgement about the most likely answer. The test works well. It combines a number of the skills used in the Graduate Management Admission Test, but is a little less detailed.

I hope you now have a sense of the way tests are put together and of their limitations. Anyone who believes that your IQ score is the final word on how well you will perform is naïve. The test can only reveal some of your abilities. The more you know about your weaknesses, the more you are likely to be able to compensate – and explain – when you are interviewed.

*Answers to the questions that appear on pp. 48–9 are as follows:
(1) Lotus=Komala, Lovely=Monoharam. (2) Ore or Out. (3) Lash, there may also be others. (4) Out. (5) About. (6) Ball. (7) Polo, Pool. (8) False. (9) Omesal=Salome (Byron, Keats, Wordsworth, Milton). Salome is not a poet. (10) Rubste=Buster (Verdi, Mozart, Chopin, Beethoven). Buster is not a composer. (11) Egrife=Fergie (Dali, Magritte, Matisse, Picasso). Fergie is no artist; the others are.*

*Answers to the questions that appear on pp. 52–3 are as follows:
(1) Margaret. (2) Yes. (3) 3+2+3=8; 11−6+8−4=9. (4) 7643. (5) Circle A=243; Circle B=32. (6) 16, 23. (7) 144 or 224. (8) 16 or 59. (9) $\frac{18}{20}$.*

Answers to the questions on pp. 55–6 are as follows:

(1)

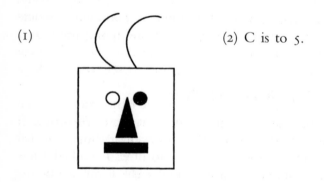

(2) C is to 5.

5. **Personality tests**

Consider, if you are going for a job, one key question: Why do you want it? Consider, if you work in personnel, the reverse key question: What qualities do you want for the job?

Unlike IQ tests, personality tests try to answer the subtle questions of what you are like. It is all about giving the right impression and that is something you can manipulate. You cannot fake brains but you can fake attitude.

You can do some jobs only if you have the ability. If you are a brilliant physicist, you may annoy people if you are rude but your personality will not affect your ability to work out new equations. Most jobs are not so cerebral. To do them well you need to have the ability and also the right personality.

In 1990, I had to take over a shop which sold greeting cards and posters. My tenant in the shop was going bankrupt. The recession had crippled him: he just could not carry on. I was obliged to pay the rent on the shop. With no tenant in place, I had no alternative but to run the shop so that I could meet the rent.

I knew that I had the wrong personality to run a shop. I could be nice to customers for a few minutes but then I would become impatient, especially if they were agonizing over a birthday card, as if it were a Picasso. I wanted to say 'You've got thirty seconds to buy or I'm not going to sell you anything ever.' The perfect selling technique!

Aware of my limitations, I got someone rather more tolerant to run the shop. Pam managed to smile at those who couldn't make up their mind what to buy and even at those who left without buying anything. From time to time, I worked a few hours in the shop. It confirmed how right I was about my personality. I got all too easily irritated. Since I was the boss, I was in the lucky position of being smart enough not to hire myself.

Success in a job depends often as much on personality as on intelligence – especially when you have to deal with the public.

Again, take stock of your own strengths and weaknesses.

EXERCISE

Potential strengths

- Like dealing with people
- Not shy
- Enthusiastic
- Persistent in sorting out problems
- Clear long-term goals
- Stable
- Enjoy sorting out people's problems
- Take criticism well.

Potential weaknesses

- Easily made anxious
- Lapse into silence easily
- Not very motivated
- Don't care which job you do
- Hate being criticized
- Hate dealing with difficult people.

Any kind of personality test is not about right or wrong answers, but about finding out more about yourself, and about conveying the impression you want to convey.

Not everyone will be able to describe their personality well but the list above is a start to help you think about what you are like. This should help you work out what kind of job you should go for. For example, if you get bored doing routine work, being a clerk is likely to make you feel unhappy and to give you little job satisfaction. Personality tests can help avoid a mismatch between the demands of the job and your own needs.

Medieval personalities

In the Middle Ages, writers outlined certain basic personality types. There were four basic types: fiery, watery, the phlegmatic, and the airy. It was very much a matter of what star you were born under. We find an echo of that in horoscopes today. They assure readers, for example, that Sagittarians are fiery, enthusiastic and very sincere, while Taureans are earthy and cautious.

The medieval scheme of personality types didn't have any science to back it up. But, since 1920, psychologists have devised tests of personality. Underlying all these tests is the belief that individuals normally have a consistent personality. If I am timid on Tuesday, I will be timid on Saturday. In the last 50 years, a mix of improved statistical techniques and better-designed questionnaires have led to more effective personality tests. Tests cover the weird and wonderful. I could show you a questionnaire which claims to predict whether you have the personality to fit into a basketball team, whether you have a mature enough personality for marriage and whether you are the right type to enjoy dirty jokes.

Most psychologists accept that our personalities stay pretty consistent unless we are going through a difficult or dramatic phase in our lives. Not all aspects of personality can be measured – every individual has odd unique quirks – but those that psychologists can quantify are known as *traits* and the theories behind them are known as *trait theories*.

Psychologists have had some success in developing trait theories. The most serious research has been spearheaded by Raymond Cattell in America and by the late Hans Eysenck in the UK. Both devised questionnaires which ask people to report on their behaviours, feelings and attitudes. From their answers, the psychologists extract patterns of responses. Analyse the patterns and you get a score for an individual on different personality traits. The most studied are extroversion/introversion and neuroticism. The tests for some traits have been well validated and are, in many ways, very solid.

Quirks and sharks

Analysing personality has always also offered rich pickings to mavericks and charlatans. Much research is trivial and far less solid than that of Eysenck and Cattell. In part this is a response to the needs of the market. There is a hunger for tests of some characteristics.

In 1973, two psychologists called Odams and Smithers published a critique of a test called the Morrisby Differential Test Battery which was being sold all over the world with 'relevant' manuals. Odams and Smithers took special exception to some of the typical profiles that went with the Morrisby Test. These 'profiles' gave a personality description based on the answers given. The manuals warned that writing backwards well showed you were more likely to be delinquent. Odams and Smithers found that in one northern town many companies used the Morrisby. Would-be apprentices went to so many sessions they became skilled at backward writing – and promptly didn't get hired because they were labelled delinquents. Morrisby thundered that Odams and Smithers, both highly respected academic psychologists, had no right to comment on this test because they hadn't been on a course that he ran and so weren't qualified! The Morrisby test has now been improved to take into account some of these criticisms.

The Morrisby episode is not the only one. In a book I co-authored with Douglas Shelley, we picked out for criticism the Rathaus Assertiveness Scale (on page 77 I explain why). It is one of literally hundreds of tests that leave a lot to be desired. They give the impression of having been thrown together quickly; often they have been tried out on peculiar and unrepresentative samples. (We found one questionnaire on sexual attitudes had been largely tested on nuns!) The evidence is that many personality tests are not very reliable and do not correlate with anything at all.

Personnel officers face a crucial problem here. They will be offered a whole range of tests often without having impartial information that allows them to judge how good these tests are. In some cases, too, you need a very sophisticated grounding in test theory to judge whether the test on offer has any merit.

TIP

*For personnel officers. Before using a personality test, assemble
as much information on its background as possible. In particular,
look out for:*

- *how reliable it is;*
- *what kinds of samples have been used to research it. Many tests
  are designed and then tested only on undergraduates because*

these are the easiest group to use. A test that works well for highly educated people in their early twenties may actually be meaningless for workers in industry;

- *what claims are being made for its validity. Is there any evidence which suggests that scoring well on the test predicts behaviour in industry?*

For people who are taking tests, personality tests present a difficult problem. You are more likely to feel that tests like this are trying to unlock your secrets – and you are right. The temptation is to be defensive.

Personality factors

The personality test you are most likely to get as part of a job interview is a test based on the Eysenck Personality Inventory (EPI) or on the Cattell 16PF scales. The Cattell 16PF Test is probably the most thorough of all. It has hundreds of questions from which are derived scores on the following scales:

Cool, Reserved v Warm Easy-going
Concrete thinking v Abstract thinking
Easily upset v Calm stable
Not assertive v Dominant
Sober, Serious v Enthusiastic
Expedient v Conscientious
Shy, Timid v Venturesome
Tough-minded v Sensitive
Trusting v Suspicious
Practical v Imaginative
Forthright v Shrewd
Self-assured v Self-doubting
Conservative v Experimenting
Group-oriented v Self-sufficient
Undisciplined v Self-disciplined
Relaxed v Tense, Driven.

Scores on some of these scales correlate together so usually if you do a 16PF scale you come out with a set of five second-order or higher factors which are:

Extroversion
Anxiety
Tough Poise
Independence
Control

The 16PF is one of the most comprehensive psychological tests. A person's scores on these various traits give a fairly rounded picture of their personality. Nevertheless, it would not reveal many qualities: how ambitious they are; whether they are likely to give up going on a business trip if their grandmother is dying.

As with the full-scale Wechsler IQ test, few companies will give job-seekers a full-scale 16PF. Most employers when they think of personality tests think of something simpler. In this chapter, I want to look at three personality traits, and how they are tested, in some detail:

- extroversion/introversion
- levels of anxiety
- assertiveness.

I want also to look at a short and widely used American test which tries to see whether you have the personality of a leader, and at one which examines the kinds of job that might suit different types. Finally I want to look at a technique that is often used – choosing colours – which claims to reveal a good deal about personality.

Does the idea of talking to strangers make you feel funny?

It is easy to see why many employers want to know whether candidates for some jobs are extroverts or introverts. Many jobs need you to be able to persuade people to buy something or to adopt a particular course of action. If you are very shy and not assertive, you are not likely to shine in such occupations.

Traditionally, Eysenck argues that there is a continuum for both these traits. No one is wholly introvert or wholly extrovert. The same would go for all other personality traits. These are the kinds of quesitons you find in these tests:

TYPICAL QUESTIONS

1. Do you enjoy talking to strangers?
2. Do you see yourself as shy?
3. Do you like going to parties?
4. Do you dislike meeting new people?
5. Do you get bored easily?
6. Do you like detailed work?
7. Do you find it easy to concentrate on work like proof-reading?
8. Are you a perfectionist?
9. Do you find you worry repeatedly over small things?
10. Do you never lie?
11. Do friends sometimes say you're a show-off?
12. Do you wish you were more persuasive?
13. Do you find it is hard to embarrass yourself?

There are some serious problems with the extroversion/introversion scale. First, it assumes that people will tell the truth about themselves. Second, many of the questions oblige you to make a choice. You either like or you don't like parties. This is not too realistic. I usually like going to parties if I think that I am going to meet interesting (or, I might as well admit it, useful) people there. On a Saturday night if I have been invited somewhere, much will depend on how I feel; if I have had to write all day, I am much less likely to go out. To enjoy a party, you have to be ready to make an effort, to chat, to buzz. The questions in the Eysenck Personality Inventory (EPI) do not allow one to make these realistic distinctions.

Extroverts tend to be more socially confident and adept than introverts. Fine for salesmen, less crucial if you want to join the research department of a firm of stockbrokers.

Introverts on the other hand tend to be more careful and methodical, which means they are likely to be good at quite demanding jobs like doing research, but also at more routine work like bookkeeping.

TIP

You can see what the questions are getting at. If you want to present yourself in a particular way, make sure that you don't overdo it. Anyone who is experienced in scoring tests will be wary of someone who scores excessively high in any personality trait. Watch in particular because a well designed test will cover the same ground twice. For example, if there is a question, 'Do you like going to parties?' there is also likely to be a question of the sort, 'Do you often dislike social gatherings?'

Try not to contradict yourself. Or if you do, be ready to explain why in your interview.

How anxious do you get?

The Eysenck neuroticism scale essentially taps the level of anxiety that people feel. Again it is not very hard to see why employers want to know about this – especially if the job involves a good deal of pressure. The kinds of questions included in the EPI that examine how anxious you are offer some insight into that.

TIP

Anxiety is more of a problem than most personality traits. Some jobs call for extroverts, some for introverts but very few call for being neurotic. The job of being Woody Allen is already taken. If you are prone to high anxiety, you should try to take some positive steps to cope with that. Blurting out how tense you feel will not go down well in most job interviews especially if you are trying to explain your test scores. The positive steps outlined in chapter 2 should help you to start to cope with your anxiety.

Asserting yourself

A third quality that employers often want is the ability to be assertive. A number of tests try to establish that ability. These tests are often tricky and many are very badly designed.

The tricky part of such tests lies in deciding just how much assertiveness is desirable. When does assertive (which is generally positive) become being aggressive (which is negative and may drive customers away)? In some occupations, the last thing you want is someone who is likely to throw their weight around. But if you want someone to represent your company at a conference, you don't want an executive who does not dare open his or her mouth. These are all subtle issues.

Questions to watch for:

- Tests which include questions within general personality tests. They will often have scales. This kind of question is difficult.

  On a seven-point scale, state how assertive you think you are: Very assertive, More assertive than most, Quite assertive, Averagely assertive, Less assertive than most, Not at all assertive, Find it very hard to be assertive.

The problem is that you need to judge whether the company wants someone who is very assertive or whether they will fear that such a person may cause trouble.

- Some employers may not rely on straight questions but use projective tests. If you are asked to say what comes into your head when you see a Blob, restrain your imagination unless you are very confident.
- One test, the Rathaus Assertiveness Test, which is sometimes used, includes the following questions which can be traps.

  1. Most people seem to be more aggressive and assertive than I am.

What happens if you are assertive but not aggressive – how do you answer?

  2. If a famed and respected lecturer makes a statement which I think is incorrect, I will have my say.

The question tells you nothing about the context. It is one thing to have your say at a committee meeting; it is quite another to interrupt a speaker who is giving a lecture. Does the company want to hire a heckler?

The test also includes a very tricky question:

  3. I am open and frank about my feelings.

In what situations? Always? Is that a good thing?

The test was researched entirely on undergraduates and seems to be much more about whether people are nice than about whether they are assertive. Being nice means not yelling. Being assertive does not mean yelling but firmly, politely and persuasively making your point.

If you are confronted with a test that appears illogical or weird, it is probably not wise to refuse to do it but it may be sensible politely to raise some of the issues if you are interviewed.

How Jung are you?

One of the most popular tests now is the Myers Briggs test. This test is based on the psychology of Carl Jung, a psychoanalyst who was Freud's apprentice and later his rival. Jung developed a complex theory of personality. Myers and Briggs adapted his ideas to create a test. They claim the more insight individuals have into their own character, the more effective they will be. That's hard to quarrel with.

The Myers Briggs test claims to place people within four dimensions. These are:

- extroversion versus introversion – are you someone for whom the outer world is important or the inner world?
- sensing versus intuition – are you someone who trusts information from your senses or from inside yourself?
- thinking versus feeling – do you think things through rationally or do you trust your feelings?
- judging versus perceiving – do you rely on your senses or intellectual judgement or more on feeling and intuition?

The publishers of the test jealously guard its contents. At the University of London Library, for example, you can only get to read the test if the psychology librarian approves you as a fit and proper person to see it.

The test consists of over a hundred statements, such as:

Which of the following is the way you most often act or feel?

1. When you have a serious choice to make do you:
   a almost always come to a clear-cut decision?
   b sometimes find it so hard to decide that you do not whole-heartedly follow up either choice?

2. Is it higher praise to say someone has:

a vision?
b common sense?

3. Are you at your best:
    a when dealing with the unexpected?
    b when following a carefully worked out plan?

The test also asks you to tick which of a series of pairs of words you prefer. You have to choose between words like imaginative or matter-of-fact, foundation or spire, impulse or decision – and about 40 others.

The questions tend to focus on whether you have faith in reason, trust your feelings, like or dislike routines, like or dislike impulsivity and are sociable or inward-looking.

It isn't too difficult to work out what is the right answer depending on what job you're going for. If you are trying to get work as an admin clerk, it's probably wise to say you like routines, prefer common sense to vision and are devoted to accuracy. If you're applying to an advertising agency as a creative type, accentuate the intuition, the original freethinker in your soul.

The Myers Briggs test claims to help managers to be particularly aware of key aspects of the way they look at – and feel about – the world. There is a serious literature on Myers Briggs which warns the test needs careful interpretation and is probably better suited to career guidance and development within companies. The publishers, however, provide potted profiles designed to help employers and human resource staff decide which individuals will fit particular jobs well.

Remember the four dimensions I described. If you are a Sensing plus Thinking type, you like facts and are impersonal in the way you handle them. You will do well in business, production and construction. If you are a Sensing plus Feeling person you will succeed in patient care, teaching and sales, apparently. Lumping these professions together seems a bit odd. How many good sales staff would make caring nurses?

As an Intuition and Feeling person you will do well in literature or psychology – and certainly not bookkeeping. (The poet T. S. Eliot, who worked much of his life as a bank clerk in foreign exchange, might have baffled Myers Briggs.) If Intuition and Thinking are your strengths, you should do well in theoretical physics, management and analysis.

The potted profiles seem a bit basic. But the test may have a more serious flaw. Many psychologists believe Jung's theories are wrong and that Jung himself had the ethics of Al Capone. Jung's character matters because the test derives some of its authority and mystique from its link with a 'great' psychoanalyst.

Jung loved to pose as a wise guru. In fact, he behaved unethically with many patients – he slept with more than a few. One of them, Sabina Spielrein, committed suicide afterwards. Jung was also a Nazi sympathizer, partly because he never came to terms with his own jealousy of Freud, who was Jewish. The reason was very personal.

Jung resented the fact that Freud refused to let him interpret one of his dreams. Freud was the father of analysis. No one, not even his brightest disciple, could probe Freud's psyche. Around 1913 Jung and Freud fell out. Their subsequent correspondence was bitter and some of it is still kept under wraps by both sides.

There is good evidence for a personality dimension like the extroversion–introversion one but the evidence for Jung's other dimensions is more questionable. Crucially many people are rational and still trust their intuition.

The review of the Myers Briggs test published in Test Critiques in the USA also points out that most studies of how reliable the test is were conducted on university students. The review published by the British Psychological Society insists the test is more useful for career guidance than job selection.

You won't please most employers by offering them an analysis of the weak points of the test. But it's one of those tests which claim to help you look into your hidden depths and you should remember that it really doesn't do that.

For those taking the Myers Briggs

The test is now scored by computer. You don't tick your answers. Each choice has a circle.

Tip one. If you don't pencil the whole circle in, the computer may score you wrong. Make sure you fill in the whole circle neatly.

Ironically, filling in 160 circles neatly and completely is the kind of task introverts do well at – and extroverts do badly at.

Tip two. *Think through the likely and obvious desirable characteristics for the job you are going for. Make your answers conform to that. It really is a test you can fake on without too many problems – and amuse yourself with the thought that most psychologists think Jung was a brilliant fraud.*

Better yet, the test is quite simple. It doesn't seem to have any questions designed to trip up those who take it.

For personnel professionals

Tip one. *The test can have its uses in team building. A good team shouldn't have too many careful, always-follow-the-rule types and no intuitives. But remember it is really quite easy to fake.*

People, theories or things

Fitting the personality you have to the right job is never just a matter of paper and pencil questions. Some tests try quite explicitly to see how well people with different personalities will do at certain jobs. One of these is the Hilson Personnel Profile/ Success Quotient.

The instructions for the test reflect some of the problems of personality testing. They state that the test asks 'how you usually feel about yourself and your life'. They go on to ask 'Please try to be as honest as possible.'

The questions are interesting because they reveal some of the wiles of psychologists:

1. Most of the time in school I have been either an average or slightly below average student.
2. I have always gotten my work done on time.
3. I do not talk about people behind their backs.
4. I have usually been in the top ten per cent of my class.
5. I have never done anything reckless.
6. I know I am much more confident in my abilities than most of my friends are in theirs.
7. I usually stayed with the popular crowd in high school.
8. I know I tend to concentrate harder on my work than others do.
9. I tend to do better under pressure of competition.

10. I have often been the leader or assistant leader in a group of friends.
11. I have never received a special award for my performance or talents at school.
12. I have never argued with a teacher.
13. I have never taken something that does not belong to me in my life.
14. I have always achieved more than my fellow classmates.

The Hilson test overlaps with some issues I deal with in the chapter on attitude since some questions aim to find out how ambitious and competitive you are. Some of its questions are straightforward. It tries to get you to be honest about school qualifications, for example. But some questions are much trickier.

The test has some well-crafted safeguards. Its designers are well aware of the fact that people will be tempted to put down all their positive traits, so they have included *candour* items. These are items which tempt you to project yourself as too good to be true. If you tick answers that make it seem no one has ever criticized you for anything and that you do not even have any minor faults, the likelihood is that you are lying. It is hard to believe, for example, that anyone has never − as question 5 invites you to say − done anything reckless in their lives.

The Hilson test is not a fully fledged integrity test. These are becoming more popular in both industry and public services.

Integrity tests

Since 2000, there have been a number of corporate scandals, like Enron, and many complaints about the behaviour of individual police officers and social workers. In a study of integrity, Kevin Murphy of the University of Pennsylvania has found that corporate corruption in the USA accounts for $100–$200 billion per year, and this vast figure excludes major accounting and investment frauds such as Enron ($60 billion) and WorldComm ($78 billion).

It's not surprising that companies want to know if you are honest, as employee theft is ten times as large a problem as street theft. Murphy estimates that prices in the USA are 15 per cent higher than they need be because of employee theft.

Equally, those who work with law enforcement and children are increasingly being asked about their ethics. Alarmed by the number of child abusers working in social services, one local authority commissioned psychologists to come up with a test where suspected paedophiles were asked if they had sexual fantasies about children. Truly dangerous paedophiles are not likely to admit this. The difficulty for personnel departments is that, while they can insert trick questions to smoke out idiots who say they never lie, most integrity and reliability tests rely on candidates being relatively truthful about themselves.

So tests tend to ask questions about whether you have been dishonest before, what you see as being dishonest, what you would do if a senior manager asked you to do something dishonest, whether you would do as he or she says or blow the whistle. And all rely on you not lying.

One of the most widely used of these tests is the 206-item Hogan Personality Inventory, which not only measures the kind of personality dimensions we have looked at but also has a reliability scale. Kevin Murphy believes that integrity tests really do offer a good guide to someone's ethical behaviour – and that women tend to score better on these tests.

So clever integrity testing tends to do more than just ask questions: it will involve some form of discussion.

A good example of the problems was reported in the *Sun* and *The Times* after the showing of a BBC film called *The Secret Policeman*. Covert filming made clear the racist views of some police officers. The Police Training and Development Board decided that something had to be done, so they introduced questions and exercises which aimed to weed out recruits who were racist.

But even this well-meant and well-designed process had problems, as the Board reflected in section 5.3 of its report on the progress of new recruits:

Probationers

When speaking to probationers at different stages of their training programme, the Inspection Team found a clear mismatch between the virtues extolled during their training and the views and attitudes of tutor constables and other experienced colleagues. A view was expressed that 'new starters go with the flow, it's part of the police culture', and it is clear new staff are heavily influenced by events going on around them.

By March 2004, all 43 police forces in England and Wales had introduced such tests into their recruitment procedures.

TIPS

I'm afraid that the only way to deal with these sometimes clever tests and discussion exercises is to be devious yourself – and that means understanding the agenda the test-makers have. It means, these days, being very aware of your prejudices. You have to be honest with yourself. And you have to be smart in working out what it is that the testers do not want to hear. I am not suggesting that you present yourself as a saint, but I am suggesting that it may be wise to keep some opinions to yourself: if, for example, you basically believe all people of a particular ethnic group will club together and lie for one another, guard against letting that slip out.

In many ways I am uncomfortable giving that advice, but there is also a body of research which suggests that if people say something very publicly, they will come to believe it. So, ironically, by lying about your prejudices you may become less prejudiced!

Traps

Other tests incorporate checks to make sure that people do not answer questions in what they believe are desirable ways. Apart from being consistent, be careful about claiming that you have some sort of perfect personality. Be careful not to lie about qualifications which can be checked. I return to 'honesty' questions in chapter 6.

The Hilson test also makes it possible to divide people into those with a history of low, medium and high achievement. But the most interesting divisions it teases out are between those who are entrepreneurial, those who will be good at taking risks and acting the leader, those who are people-oriented and may actually be good managers, and those who are academically oriented and may be very good at background work.

Colours

One of the most attractive ideas floating around in personality research is that the colours you prefer say something fundamental about you. Like medieval theories of character, this is an old notion. Fiery people like red. There are a number of tests on the market which claim to do this. These tests are very controversial and their predictive value uncertain.

Devious designs

In many of the situations this book deals with, the crucial question is whether the tests really do predict how well people will do on the job. With personality tests, there is another issue. How much of the truth about yourself do you reveal?

Once you know about the philosophy and purpose behind some tests, it does not require genius to give the answers that you think are desired.

Many studies show psychologists get different answers depending on the instructions they give. Depending whether you ask subjects to tell the truth, or to give the answers that will look best for themselves, you get quite different responses. Many psychologists believe that people automatically do this. We like to put our best foot forward in any situation. If subjects do this in a laboratory situation, where nothing important hangs on the result, they are much more likely to do it when they want a job.

If this is a natural tendency, the best advice a book like this can give is to do it consciously, with care, and, yes, with craftiness. Put on your psychological Sunday best, but do it in a way that is convincing and that won't store up too much trouble for you either at the interview or, if you get the job, later on.

Let us suppose you are going for a job as a salesman. You do not have to be Freud to intuit that answering 'No' to the question 'Do you enjoy meeting new people?' is probably the wrong answer. As it happens, you find meeting new people quite hard.

Let us put morality to one side just for now. There are arguments both for and against giving the answer that you like meeting people.

For: You need the job. You may actually change if you start to do the job. There is evidence that people do grow into their jobs and that their personality comes to fit what they have to do.

Against: You may land yourself with a job you find very hard; people will notice. This will lead to trouble and, possibly, to a loss of self-confidence as you find you cannot do the job well.

What I hope you will have realized by now is that there is a second argument against lying. The personnel officer may be aware of all the research on social desirability. If the way you present yourself clashes with your test answers, he or she may well conclude that you have been faking. So compromise.

TIP

If you have to fake, do not fake too much and fake intelligently. Be consistent in the way you present your character and do not fall into the trap of portraying yourself as an out-and-out extrovert if you know that the moment you get into an interview situation, you are going to twitch, stammer and get tongue-tied.

There is a quite clever strategy I have known people to use. They go into the interview saying, for example, that they used to be shy but that they are now working on it. In some ways, this is an impressive answer because it shows both insight and determination to improve oneself to fit in with what the company wants. The risk is whether you will impress if you draw attention to any of your weaknesses.

Personality testing is a more imprecise art than IQ testing. Personnel officers need to research the tests they intend to use. And those who take tests must remember that experienced testers know people cannot fake IQ answers. You need to be careful to make sure that the picture you put over of yourself is not too rosy to be believed – and that it does not conflict too obviously with the way you behave.

6. Tests of creativity

Imagine a scene. It is 1840 and Charles Dickens is seeking work. He is not yet a world-famous writer. His employer sits him down and gives him a test to complete. Dickens' answers, the would-be employer informs him, will reveal whether he is really creative.

The scene sounds absurd but, in fact, it isn't entirely so. Psychologists have been using tests to see how creative people are for nearly 60 years.

Creativity tests are popular but paradoxical. Popular because companies increasingly want to know that they are hiring creative people who can come up with new ideas in a fast-changing business environment. Paradoxical because to be creative is to throw up new, original and often challenging ideas, whereas tests usually ask fairly mundane questions. As we saw in the chapter on personality, tests may not require a right answer but they usually ask for the opposite of imaginative answers.

If a test question asks, 'Do you like parties?', it usually requires a Yes or No answer. At best, a test may allow some form of 'Maybe' or 'Sometimes'. None of this makes it possible to cope with a response such as, 'I like parties where there is soul music, plenty of vodka and girls in black leather. I hate parties where grease heads go on about their motorbikes.' A simple Yes/No format can't manage such subtlety. But tests are created when there is demand for them. Increasingly industry wants to know whether some potential recruits can offer new ideas.

So tests for creativity are a paradox. Creativity is no longer just something great writers, painters or great inventors – Dickens, Van Gogh or Marconi – achieve. Today, every occupation aspires to be creative. Creative cooks cater for creative accountants who need the skills of creative computer programmers – possibly to cook the books!

When many workers were essentially just doing a specific and regimented task on an assembly line, no one wanted creativity. Attitudes have changed, on the surface at least. There are companies that charge huge fees for advising businesses on company logos or the names of brands. First they dream up a name, then they research its various associations.

To get into the spirit of this chapter, I want readers to imagine the least appropriate name they can think of for a new brand of chocolate. My choices include Dark Mud, Scum, Muck. And I'm being polite. Anyway, creativity is in fashion and can be hugely profitable.

Being creative in terms of psychological testing is not quite like being creative in real life. It does not mean being able to write or paint masterpieces. In a previous chapter, I pointed out that there was a difference between *convergent* thinking and *divergent* thinking. Convergers are good at answering questions which have precise answers; divergers may score much less well on those but are good at producing a flow of ideas.

Convergers are not better or smarter than divergers. And divergers are not smarter or better than convergers. It is a question of cognitive style. By and large, in psychological testing, creativity means being a divergent thinker.

In this chapter I want to look at four kinds of creative tests:

- Tests of production of ideas. The idea is to see how fluent you are at churning out one idea after another. This is not some bizarre academic ritual. It is exactly what executives often do in brainstorming sessions.
- Tests which see how well people find connections between unlikely objects or themes. A great deal of advertising and marketing depends on pictures and copy which hit just such unlikely links.
- Visual tests – especially tests of the ability to spot and, sometimes, to create visual puns, and tests of the ability to create a story around a picture.
- Tests of lateral thinking. Lateral thinking is a phrase invented by the psychologist Edward de Bono. In the late 1960s, he argued that very often people look at problems in only one way and, therefore, plump for the most obvious solution. Lateral thinking offers a set of techniques for more devious

and original thinking. De Bono's ideas have had a considerable impact on industry.

Since many people do not think of themselves as creative, I also ask whether or not it is possible to teach people to be creative. I certainly do not think it is possible to teach someone to be a great writer or artist: that either comes or it doesn't. But there is considerable evidence which suggests that you can teach some of the creative and 'lateral' skills that these tests are after.

EXERCISE

Again, as before, think of your strengths and weaknesses. Here are some points to set you thinking.

- Like making things up
- Like strange drawings
- Think creative people odd
- Prefer facts
- Find it hard to think of new ideas
- Originality is for really clever people
- Can't see the point of clever puns
- Scared of looking foolish.

Fluency of ideas

Many theories of thinking stress that thinking involves the association of ideas. If you think 'table', the next thought is often likely to be 'chair'. What creativity tests test very much depends on making up – and, in some cases, spotting – less than obvious associations. 'Table' may suggest 'chair' to you but it could also suggest 'billiards' (billiard tables) and 'water' (water table). Creativity tests can be fun.

Uses of objects

One of the most frequently used tests is the Uses of Objects test which was devised by J. P. Guildford in 1954. Guildford got people to imagine many different uses for objects. His favourite objects were a brick, a match and a toothpick. There is no reason, however, why one should be limited to just these objects.

How many uses can you think of for a brick? How many uses can you think of for a match? The convergent thinker will tend to come up with literal uses such as using a brick to build a house or using a match to light a fire. What else would a sensible person do with a match or brick? Such answers reveal a lack, not necessarily of effective imagination but of playfulness. Under pressure, convergent thinkers may well just repeat the basic use.

Creative thinking needs flexibility. Good answers to the use of a brick would include:

- to build a house
- to build a wall
- to build an oven
- as a violent weapon
- as a hammer to bash nails in
- as a work of art – sell it to the Tate
- as a dinner table for mice
- to break a window
- to balance another brick on scales
- to help secure a ladder.

Think of a few ideas for yourself. Here are some other objects to muse about: a balloon, a helmet, a table, a wig. And musing is the right word. The ability to dream up unusual uses for objects may come naturally to some people but, actually, it isn't that hard. Part of the trick is in getting rid of one's inhibitions that make one believe some options are too silly to write down.

The wig is interesting because, unlike all the other objects, it is divisible. You can remove individual threads of hair. This opens up many interesting new possibilities. For example, any individual hair can be used, as in the James Bond movies, as your own personal security measure. You stick one in front of your briefcase; if it is not there when you get back from champagne at the casino, you know the opposition has been at your secret papers. A wig could also make a tea cosy.

The Uses of Objects game can be fun if you are a divergent thinker. But there is a tendency for people to get stuck and to keep on repeating one basic use such as using a match:

- to light a fire

- to light a cigarette
- to light a stove.

One of the problems with the way the test is scored by those who don't really understand it properly is that they will count such repetitive ideas as being as 'good' as new ideas, such as using a match to prop your eyelids open after a heavy night's drinking.

In general, the Uses of Objects test is more fun than most others. I have been in groups when the ideas produced get wilder and more eccentric. The trouble is that often many of the ideas suggested are wholly useless. You would have to be a real banana-brain to use a wig as a tea cosy. So while it is creative to dream up such a use, you also need to make sure that the person who suggested it knows how silly it is.

Critical assessment

When the Uses of Objects test is given in an academic exercise, testers rarely ask people to justify how they would use the objects. Often in recruitment, personnel officers will ask people going for jobs to take the exercise in a slightly different way. Individuals will be asked to join in a group. The group will be set a task or a problem and have to come up with all kinds of solutions. I look into this sort of game more in the chapter on role-playing, but there are good reasons for looking at some aspects of it here while dealing with creativity.

Brainstorming usually involves three distinct phases:

1. An introduction in which the nature of the problem you are going to brainstorm is set out.

2. The storming phase in which either the individual or the group throws out as many ideas as possible about how to solve the problem. It is this phase which has the most similarities with the Uses of Objects test.

3. A critical assessment phase in which you try to see how practical all the ideas are that you came up with in 2.

Let us suppose that you are going for a job in the marketing department of a company. They have adapted the Uses of Objects test to their own specific situation. They ask potential employees to throw up marketing ideas to sell a new brand of car. They stress the ideas can be as silly or exotic as you like.

You produce eight different ideas including advertising the car by getting people to run naked into the fountains at Trafalgar Square where they drape themselves with togas that are painted with the Logo Model X. Original it certainly is; practical it is not!

It is important to be able to judge which wild ideas have some merit in being followed up and which were just sparked off on the spur of the moment. Trying to convince a group of the genius of six really daft ideas which you came up with is likely to put them off seeing why your two good, practical ideas should be taken further.

TIP

Again, it is important in any such exercise to be able to see the difference between the wildly creative phase of having lots of ideas and the critical phase of eliminating the useless ones. Anyone who writes will know exactly what I mean. First you dream and then you shape, polish, re-shape. This is as creative a process as anything else.

It is easy, of course, to quantify responses to the Uses of Objects test. The score is simple; how many uses did each subject dream up? It is much harder to work out how good each of the ideas was.

Spotting associations

As I argued in the chapter on intelligence, we tend to think through associations. One favourite form of question is to ask people to think of as many meanings as they can for words which have multiple uses. For example:

How many meanings can you think of for:
pitch
bear

mean
turn?

All these words have a variety of meanings.

The second kind of test is, in some ways, the reverse of the Uses test. Subjects are given a set of apparently quite different objects, themes or activities. They then have to spot the hidden link between these. One form of this is the Remote Associates test.

This test presumes creative people will be able to spot connections that the less gifted would not be able to see. Typical questions ask people to spot the link between Switzerland, the moon and mice. The answer is *cheese*. Switzerland is famous for cheese; the moon was once said to be made of cheese; mice are supposed to love cheese.

Another question is to find the link between life, number, Greenwich. The answer is *prime* because you have the phrase 'the prime of life', there are prime numbers, and the Prime Meridian runs through Greenwich.

It is fairly obvious success in a test like this depends not just on pure creativity but also on a considerable amount of cultural knowledge.

Here are five other examples of what is basically the same kind of question. It is something that crossword addicts can excel at.

wheel – electric – high
mouse – blue – cottage
pepper – girl – East
surprise – line – birthday
window – mortgage – ware
(For the answers to these questions, see p. 97)

TIPS

Tip one. *Do not get stuck with thinking it is impossible.*

Tip two. *Choose the word of the trio that feels most familiar to you and rattle through the associations that you have to it. You may suddenly think 'Eureka'.*

There are other associative tests including one curious test in which people are asked to give as many possible words that rhyme with a given word.

Both the uses of objects and the various associative tests focus essentially on verbal creativity. As far as I know there are no creative number tests. But there certainly are many visual tests of creativity.

Creative images

A picture speaks a thousand words is the saying. We live in a society in which images are very important. It is not just the obvious tasks – packaging, advertising, marketing – that demand visual skills. I recently bought a new vacuum cleaner. It came with a very smart pamphlet with illustrations that explained everything one might ever want to know about how a vacuum cleaner works. The never-ending stream of electronic gadgets and computers also needs to be technically written up so that consumers can understand them. It is not surprising that more employers than ever before are keen to hire people who have a good visual sense. One of the most famous advertising images was that of a pregnant man. The accompanying copy said 'Would you use a contraceptive if it was you that got pregnant?'

Tests of visual creativity want to see whether people can understand and come up with such visual games. There are tests which require a visual response like:

Fill in the blanks in the following sequence of pictures.

A second kind of test tries to see how well people will connect language and picture. They depict a situation and then ask subjects to make up a story that explains the situation. This is also used in tests of attitude and motivation. What marks out creativity tests is that they usually offer an ironic or surrealistic picture.

The Torrance Test of Creative Thinking, for example, has one picture in which Jerry has got the better of Tom. It shows a canary who appears to have gobbled up a cat. At least, the giant-toothed bird has a cat's tail hanging out of its mouth. There is a forlorn 'meow' coming out of the canary's mouth. Discuss. This is not the kind of essay you get set for a GCSE.

A second picture is called the Ant who Overate. I happen to think it's a very disappointing picture. The ant is bloated and he does have normal-sized ants in his burrow. But it is a picture that is much less interesting than the canary one. I think one of the only ways to develop a story is to give the ant an unhappy family background as a result of which he developed an eating disorder.

Some creative tests are just nice visual puzzles like this one.

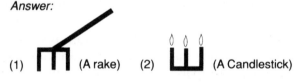

Such tests are obviously playful and that is one nice thing about them. But, in general, the companies that give them are not at all light-hearted about seeking creativity. The right slogan, the right packaging can make all the difference between the success and failure of a product.

De Bono

One psychologist who has been very active in promoting a new view of creative thinking is Edward De Bono, the author of popularized lateral thinking, and more recently, *Po*. Much of what De Bono has to say is very sane and a good counter to rigid thinking.

De Bono argues that there is too much emphasis on convergent intelligence. He warns of the dangers of complacency and arrogance. Industry and politics both need a much more imaginative and almost poetic approach. *Po* stands for both *po*ssible, hyp*o*thesis and *po*etic. What paralyses many people is the fear of being wrong, De Bono claims.

Many companies have been influenced by De Bono's ideas and lateral thinking exercises are often tried. In lateral thinking, as in many kinds of brainstorming, there is no shame in dreaming up daft ideas. First, you flow; then you evaluate.

De Bono stresses that lateral thinking tries to find roundabout solutions and even solutions that may raise new problems. He highlights using ideas as stepping stones and advises challenging accepted concepts. He has also devised the notion of exlectics which involves trying to isolate what is the key feature of any situation.

De Bono offers a critique of how psychologists look at intelligence and creativity and also a sort of inspirational system for companies. To explain his ideas in detail is not possible in a short book but it is worth looking at one of his experiments to get a flavour of his theory. The Black Cylinder Experiment is suitably dramatic.

People come into a room in which there is a black cylinder on a table. After a while, the cylinder falls over for no apparent reason. They have to explain why it did so.

This is an interesting game. Reasons can range from:

- The cylinder is not that stable. The draught from the door blew it over.
- There is fluid inside. It has been draining away.
- There is a clockwork mechanism which makes it fall over.
- A snail has been climbing up inside one of the walls.
- Mice are inside.

There are clear links between this kind of exercise and Guildford's problems, except Dr Bono calls for much more technical skill in some exercises. The Black Cylinder problem is worth contemplating. There are no right or wrong answers, just interesting hypotheses. After the 1997 election, the UK government promoted the image of 'cool' Britannia, whose culture industries sold worldwide. Creativity is in more demand than ever before. Remember, however, the tests I have described offer at best only a small hint of how creative someone can be – and whether they can turn that potential creativity into anything more than doodling fun. Still, by now the tests should hold fewer terrors.

Answers to the questions that appear on p. 93 are as follows:

wheel – electric – high = chair
mouse – blue – cottage = cheese
pepper – girl – East = spice
surprise – line – birthday = party
window – mortgage – ware = house

We have wheelchairs, highchairs and electric chairs. Mice eat cheese, cottage and blue are kinds of cheese. Pepper is a spice, spices come from the East, and we all know the Spice Girls. Party line, surprise party and birthday party are all familiar. Windows fit houses, you need a mortgage to buy a house and houses need housewares.

7. **Tests of attitude**

It is five o'clock on Friday afternoon. The company has an unexpected large order to fulfil by next Tuesday. Gilbert, who is a skilled tool-maker, couldn't care less. He has planned to go fishing with his mates from the pub. Come 5.15, he's off. Let the management worry about the order. That's what they are paid for.

Larry is also a skilled tool-maker but his attitude is different. He offers to work most of the weekend. It is his son's fourth birthday but, as long as he is around for the actual party, Larry doesn't mind putting in extra time. The overtime will be good. Also, he knows how vital it is for the company to fulfil this order.

The distinction between these two workers seems simple. Larry is motivated; Gilbert is not. In fact, it is not quite so straightforward. Gilbert is motivated to do many things – and not all of them are relaxing leisure activities like fishing – but his current work doesn't matter to him at all. It is just a way of making his wages. He resents it as boring and repetitive. Gilbert wishes he had gone on to college. He dreams of becoming a graphic designer. His sense of identity does not depend on how he does his factory work. If the company had known Gilbert would be so unmotivated, it probably wouldn't have hired him.

Many psychologists admit it is hard to devise good tests of motivation but there is a growing feeling that, with more sophisticated techniques and a sharper eye for fake answers that flatter, employers can assess the motivation of recruits more accurately.

EXERCISE

Again it is useful for you to list what you see as your strengths and weaknesses.

Potential strengths
- Ambitious
- Clear long-term goals
- Lots of drive
- Not frightened of going for it
- Honesty
- Good degree of self-knowledge.

Weaknesses
- No clear long-term goals
- A tendency to exaggerate
- Often don't finish things
- Not much energy for work.

Motivation is very individual. Some theories divide people into highly motivated as against quite unenergetic individuals, but much depends on the specific task in hand. Gilbert will travel for six hours to get some good trout fishing, so it is not that he lacks drive, he just lacks drive for this job. Second, the political climate matters.

Think of attitudes in the 1980s. In Britain under Mrs Thatcher and in America under President Reagan it was politically correct to be a workaholic. Millionaires sprouted like mushrooms in a damp forest. Financial success was chic. Then many people wondered if they were right to give up so much for work. Many executives questioned putting work ahead of their family life and their hobbies. Today, with the emphasis Tony Blair's government puts on the need to work, the pendulum has swung back. There are, for example, 1,270 schemes in Europe whose aim is to motivate disadvantaged – or lazy – youngsters to work.

Yet motivation is a key factor in how well people are likely to do in a job. Companies therefore want to know about the drive level and attitudes of recruits. And even here things have become more complex. With fraud and financial scandals so much in the news, many companies now also want to get a feel for the ethics of recruits. Are they honest? Would they report irregularities if they spotted them? Too much ambition may actually be the last thing they want.

The ground covered in this chapter overlaps a little with the ground covered in the chapter on personality tests. There is, however, an important difference. Personality tests hope people will be honest but if they give dishonest answers, the test should get the truth about them. If subjects lie, the test works less well. Tests of drive, ambition and values have been created from slightly different premises. They often assume that our need to achieve involves unconscious motives. Often, we are not wholly aware of why we want to push to do things. The direct questions used in the tests I analysed in chapter 5 are too transparent to give a rounded picture, so psychologists resort to wilier means.

Projective tests

Projective tests are essentially tests in which people are given pictures and the outline of stories. They then have to complete these. Psychologists believe that these are very 'empty' stimuli; subjects start from them and the way they see the pictures or complete the stories reveals a great deal about underlying motivations.

The idea is simple. If you are shown a picture of a table and you say it is an elephant, you are either mad or joking. But if you are shown a vague form, that could be anything. It is a blank. The way you describe it says more about what you think and feel than about the object. You *project* on to it your own concerns. Hence the term *projective* techniques.

Shown this shape a rugby player might see a ball, while a good-time girl might see a ring soon to be on her finger.

Many psychologists believe projective techniques are hard to 'fake good' because they are more subtle than direct questions like, 'Are you honest?' or 'Are you unreliable?' Who would say No to the first or Yes to the second?

Projective tests have a long history and the famous ones have been extensively researched, so many personnel experts believe they offer a useful way of tapping into people's real motives and feelings. In particular, they seem to provide a way of getting at deeper levels of personality.

For job-seekers this means they have to be wary, for projective tests are full of traps. They owe a good deal to psychoanalytic ideas. The image you will have to describe or tell a story about means nothing by itself. What you say it is will reveal what you are really thinking about.

Inkblots

One of the best-known tests is the Rorschach which is basically a collection of inkblots. You have to say what the inkblot is. Consider this Blob:

There are no right or wrong answers, but let us look at what four possible answers might suggest. I can see in the Blob:

  – a bagpipe
  – a cell with dendrites
  – an organizational flow chart

or:

  – the sun and its rays.

The sun is the most obvious and safest answer. Children often draw the sun like that. If you say it is a flow chart, it looks as if you might be trying a little too hard to make a business-like impression. If you say it is a bagpipe, it suggests a sense of humour, but a weird one. A cell with dendrites sounds learned and serious so it may be the smartest answer.

The Rorschach test is controversial. Critics claim it promises more than it delivers. Experts often cannot agree what responses really mean. Some psychiatrists use it but they often disagree about whether particular responses show someone is suffering from a mental illness or is well adjusted.

In job recruitment, be careful. My own inclination if shown something like this Blob is to giggle and think up some less than obvious thing it represents. But this is a poor tactic.

TIPS

Tip one. *Take it seriously.*

Tip two. *Find a plausible but quite serious response. Unless test givers are confident and sophisticated, they do not like people being ironic about test materials.*

So resist the temptation to say the blob looks like a bagpipe or a man with an unfortunate hairdo. Plump for the cell with dendrites or, simple but serious, a wheel.

Tip three. *To make sure that subjects don't just present what they reckon those interviewing them want, some questionnaires also incorporate a few trick questions like the ones I analysed in the Hilson test. Be very careful if a follow-up question asks if you have never done anything wrong or are always committed to getting work done on time. Few of us are such paragons of capitalism. 'Never' and 'always' are dangerous responses.*

How ambitious are you?

A key question is how much achieving objectives matters to you. Psychologists argue that everyone has certain needs – a need for food, drink, sleep, sex, social approval. Some claim that most individuals in Western culture also have an achievement need which is written as *nAch*, for need for achievement.

The most used test of achievement motivation tries to quantify the achievement need different individuals have. It is just the kind of projective test I have been describing. It is called the Thematic Apperception Test, but generally goes by the more user-friendly name of TAT.

The TAT is intriguing, controversial and has a strange

history. In the 1950s, two Harvard psychologists saw that there were huge differences in economic achievement in different periods. They argued that this must have something to do with people's need to achieve. For example, Elizabethan England enjoyed a boom which was partly due to the new sea routes that were being discovered. The two psychologists, David McClelland and Richard Atkinson, wondered whether the literature of the years before it offered any clue. Did it differ in any way from what was being written at times when there was no economic boom?

The long and the short of a complex theory is that the psychologists found that about 40 to 50 years before an economic boom, the literature of that society changed. There were far more references to success and to striving; people dreamed of conquering new frontiers. They concluded that when Sir Francis Drake and the other great explorers were children, their parents were very achievement-minded and communicated that to their children.

Analysis of later periods focused on children's books and confirmed the findings. These content analyses again revealed far more achievement imagery, far more references to striving and to actual instances of achievement. A good instance of an achievement-oriented children's book is Tolkien's *The Hobbit* where Mr Bilbo Baggins, the well-known and generally idle hobbit, finds himself increasingly involved in searching for the dragon's gold and takes many risks in his endeavour.

Based on such findings, McClelland and Atkinson devised the Thematic Apperception Test. They incorporated some of the ideas that had been tried with the Inkblot test. A pack of TAT cards consists of about 30 cards, each with a picture on it. Subjects are asked to tell the story the picture illustrates. In one card, for example, a young boy is playing the violin.

People are normally asked to tell the story in about five minutes. This would be the kind of response that would indicate someone was achievement orientated: 'The young boy has been very musical since he was four. His parents bought him his first violin when he was six. He practises three hours every day because he wants to improve and hopes to go to the Conservatoire of Music.'

The kind of response that would indicate someone was not particularly achievement orientated would be: 'The boy found his violin in the corner of the house and is enjoying having a go on it. The noise drives his grandmother mad.'

The difference is clear. In the first case, the story is about success. Playing the violin is a means to an end, to a 'result'. In the second case, playing the violin is fun. The story is imaginative but it doesn't lead to any useful end.

Usually, those who give the TAT are vague in their instructions, the idea being that this should allow people's natural inclinations to come through.

Clearly, it is not as easy to fake a response to the TAT as to a question which asks if you will sacrifice everything for the company's good. Nevertheless, candidates who want to make a good impression can present themselves as bursting with ambition.

David McClelland was aware of this problem. He told me that he thought it was hard for people who were not really success-minded consistently to come up with stories in which achieving was a key element.

Tip four. *If you are going to be honest, then just tell the story that comes to your mind.*

If you want to convince the company that you are very ambitious analyse the picture, ask what could be a good outcome of the activity it depicts and use that as a start. Cram it with achievement words like 'ambitious', 'striving' and 'success' but make sure the tale is coherent and not too far-fetched.

Does the environment matter?

Much research shows that responses to TAT tests can be influenced. People will tell different stories depending on the setting in which they are being tested and the instructions that they are given. Critics claim that this is a weakness of the test, but there is now a tradition of research which shows scores on the test often do correlate with both academic success and economic achievement. This is true in societies as different as the USA and Turkey.

The TAT and the Rorschach are both classic examples of tests which should not be taken or scored in isolation. The guidelines produced by the British Psychological Society emphasize your right to feedback. If you are asked to take a test like this, you should politely ask for feedback to give you some idea of how they intend to interpret your responses.

Projective tests are not the only ones to have traps.

Analysing motives

A good example of the kind of test that is less simple than it appears is one devised at the Institute for Personality Testing. It looks very straightforward but, in fact, it has been carefully designed not to trap, but to tease out inconsistencies and people's attempts to make themselves 'look good'.

There are four kinds of questions in the test. The first asks people how they would prefer to spend either their time or their money. For example:

1. You have finished your work for the day an hour ahead of schedule. Do you:
   * start on the next day's work?
   * go home early?
   * doodle in the office imagining what tomorrow's problems may be?

2. You have just received a windfall of £1,000. Do you:
   * put it in the bank for a rainy day?
   * splash out on a holiday to the south of France?
   * use some of it to splash out but also finally now sign on for the computer course you have wanted to do for so long?
   * invest it all in computer equipment?

The next questions rely on word association. The logic is that your association should reveal what is uppermost in your mind. One example:

3. What is the first thing that comes into your mind when you hear the word CHAIR?

TABLE is so obvious here that anyone who gives another reply is either weird or trying to draw attention to themselves.

Few words, however, have such automatic associations. For example:

4. What is the first thing that comes into your mind when you hear the word TYPE?
   • Writer? Cast? Sort? Stereo?

The third sort of question asks you what you think of some statements like:

5. The way to succeed in a particular job is to amass as much information as possible about the background to the task. Is this:
   • true?
   • a little naïve?
   • not relevant?

Motivation is about priorities. If there is a conflict what do you prefer? The four kinds of questions present scenarios where no course of action is perfect.

6. I read periodicals which carry the latest news about civil engineering:
   • never
   • occasionally
   • from cover to cover
   • not when I'm into a good novel
   • selectively because much of the material is dull and irrelevant.

7. I am on a business trip. I wake up at 7 a.m. and have an hour to spare. I use it:
   • to go swimming in the hotel pool
   • to have a lie in
   • to look again at our planning for today's meeting
   • to have a large breakfast with other members of the team.

The test yields four scores:

• The individual's basic drives.

- The individual's aspirations. Just what is the limit of their ambitions?
- A score for conflict. What happens when your aspirations conflict with basic drives? How willing would you be to give up a long-awaited date if the company wants you to work late that night?
- A total motivation score – the relative energy with which a person will go for a particular goal.

Notice that the questions are indirect. They do not ask you whether you would agree or refuse to work late at night, for example. The Institute claims that this test is hard to fake because it doesn't use many direct questions. They even argue that it is harder to fake than straight projective techniques.

Tests like this which employ a variety of question-types require a great deal of concentration. You should make sure that your answers about your attitudes are consistent.

Be particularly wary of giving the impression that you will sacrifice anything for work. This looks 'too good' and may not be believed.

With reference to conflict, it is good to give the impression that you can deal maturely with dilemmas. On questions like 7, does the man who wakes at 7 a.m. and immediately gets his brain into analysing and planning turn up fresh and effective for the actual meeting? It might be wiser to go swimming or breakfast with your colleagues – a well-known bonding experience.

Too much ambition can be awkward

Ambition is not always welcome. You should think about the kind of company you are applying to. Large companies usually welcome the really ambitious. Small family-run companies may be more ambivalent. The best jobs are kept in the family. Cousin Fred will be head of sales because he is cousin Fred. Industrialists do not like to admit such companies still exist but thousands do – and may not want a driven outsider. Before you project yourself as Mr or Ms Aggressive Ambition pause and ponder the kind of outfit you are trying to join.

Self-interest

Some large companies do try to assess potential recruits – especially graduates – in considerable depth. On the whole, however, that is rare because most job assessment procedures do not have time for such self-analysis.

Some of us know from our teens what we want to do. But many clever people do not feel they were meant to be a geologist or a doctor or a merchant banker. For them, it is very useful to analyse methodically not just their motives but their interests. They might offer a clue to what their career should be.

Since the 1920s the Strong Interest Inventory has been used in vocational guidance, partly because it is so remarkably thorough. Strong put together a very long list of activities, jobs and people and asked subjects to rate if they liked, disliked or were indifferent to them. A simple technique, but the sheer scale of the test – if you manage to concentrate – suggests it gets at some truths. Strong asks for your reactions to:

- 131 occupations
- 36 school subjects
- 51 activities
- 39 amusements or hobbies
- 24 types of people.

By the time you have ticked the 281 boxes, you are likely to be tired and to have a pretty good idea of any pattern that distinguishes jobs you love from jobs you hate.

But the Strong Inventory does not stop there. Thirty questions ask people to choose whether they would prefer to do one thing, like spend time analysing their mistakes, or another, like general reading, in case that may be useful in the future.

The final part of the Inventory sets out 14 different characteristics and asks people to say whether or not they have them.

The merit of inventories like these is that they do make you think about choices and preferences. There are a number of tests which have a slight philosophical bent to try and get people to reveal their life goals. Do they want a quiet, contented life with plenty of time to potter in the garden and think deep spiritual thoughts? Or do they want the flash of success and the money that goes with that enough to drive and drive themselves?

Tip five. *This is a test in which you should be honest. There is no point in lying about this or you will find yourself in the kind of predicament Gilbert is in — doing a job he doesn't like and that he increasingly resents. You may have to settle for such a job but you should at least know what you ideally want.*

Attitudes to technology

We live in an information society and technology is changing very fast. In 1990 it was probably still just possible to get hired for office jobs without word-processing skills and with a minimum of computer literacy. Today, you'd be hard pressed.

E-commerce, business on the internet, is a major part of the Western economies. Employers want to hire people who can handle computers and the internet and who are capable of performing e-commerce. Our education system isn't providing the training we need, however. It seems like only yesterday that the magazine *New Scientist* showed that many people were intimidated by video recorders. They didn't know how to set them to record a programme for next Saturday. Video companies lovingly produced literature explaining the seven steps required to tape *Casualty* but intelligent people remained baffled by the instructions. However, video recorders now seem a piece of cake compared with trying to record something on your DVD player through your digibox.

There are two different sorts of tests you may be asked to take — tests of computer skills and tests of attitudes to new technology. Temping agencies usually ask people to word process some text and to perform basic computer operations like setting up a simple spreadsheet. These are not tricky tests of themselves but they can be intimidating if you have little experience or if you haven't done such tasks recently.

Often now the recruitment process also involves an assessment where candidates are given a project to work on. They're then sat at a computer and bombarded with on-screen messages — some relevant, some not. Some employers mix business messages with personal ones. The idea is to see how well people can focus on the job in hand and deal with a number of tasks.

Companies also want to have a sense of people's attitudes to technology and to change. They might be deciding to bring in a whole new information system. Ageism is rampant here, with many employers assuming that anyone over 40 is computer-nervous (as if over forties were educated in the days when people used quills!).

Many IQ, personality and attitude tests are available in computerized versions so you may be asked to do them at a computer terminal. This has unintended consequences. One good tactic in any test is to spend the first minute checking how many questions there are and what, in general, they're like. Some computerized tests don't allow you to scroll down to review them. Ask, if you are told tests will be on computer, if you can scroll down. A number of tests also try to gauge people's attitudes to technology. Don't be surprised if you're asked to rate how much you agree or disagree with statements like these:

- I want to get more knowledge of computers.
- I am sometimes not sure how to handle e-mail.
- I am not motivated to try hard to improve my computer skills.
- Computers are really rather alien beings.
- Everyone exaggerates the importance of new technology. Real business is done person to person.

These tests of attitude allow you to say whatever you like and, therefore, to lie, claiming to love anything computerized. Such lies won't be very convincing if your computer skills are poor, however. The trend is for more performance tests so it really is worth sharpening up your computer skills.

Tip six. *If new technology scares you, then you must work to overcome this or you will find yourself at a disadvantage in a competitive job market. Read about new technology and make yourself familiar with it. If you are currently unemployed, there are government-sponsored courses which will give you a chance to catch up on the latest developments. Most local further education colleges also run courses.*

Work style

As we understand more about motivation, we see that individuals will work well under some conditions and much less well under others. A number of tests try to get at preferences in working style, usually by getting people to rate how they feel about statements like these:

I hate to work under day-to-day supervision.
Reply: Agree strongly, Agree, Middle, Disagree, Disagree strongly.

'Values' tests claim to be able to give a much more rounded picture than most personality tests about the kind of things that matter to an individual. The best known tests in this area are tailored to the needs of industry. The Values Scale consists of 106 items. They are analysed for 21 different values, and seek to understand the need for prestige, variety and approval.

Are you a team player?

Business increasingly wants people to be team players as well as creative and competitive. Large companies often go on Away Days to plan strategies and to bond. Even the Conservative Party went on such a bonding exercise soon after William Hague became its leader. Hague used to work for management consultants McKinsey so it seemed logical to him; many of his MPs seemed a little bemused. The problem is that recruiters often want to know whether someone is going to be a team player before they let them join the team.

Tests and exercises such as the Skills Inventory For Teams are trying to cope with an impossible task. The so-called SIFT asks people who take part in team exercises to comment on how well the team has done, whether it was focused and whether team members were highly committed. Obviously if you're given a questionnaire about a team exercise after having done one, you must bear in mind what happened but beware of being too critical of other members of the team. Good team players support other members of the team; they don't blame and backbite. The safest approach is to emphasize your co-operative tendencies and to play down a little your competitive streak.

Ethics

I have advised you to be careful in how you present yourself. I rarely suggest out-and-out lying and I have argued that you should be consistent and not outrageous in the image you put forward. Many companies increasingly need to know whether executives (especially those who have the power to make important decisions) are so ambitious as to be willing to do anything to succeed. Companies obviously cannot give people lie detector tests but worry about honesty. In the United States, a number of tests have been developed which try to assess how honest people are, but the tests themselves have been attacked for invading privacy.

These tests incorporate two features – one of which is a familiar invitation to perjure oneself. On the face of it, no one can answer No to any of the following:

- Have you ever stolen a button?
- Have you ever been rude to your parents?

- Have you ever felt jealous or envious towards somebody?
- Have you ever said something behind somebody's back?

There may be occasional saints who have never committed any of these acts but be careful before you present yourself as such a saint. No one will ever believe you in the cut-throat world of industry.

The American innovation has been to devise statements which you have to agree or disagree with, like:

- The use of industrial espionage is justified if the good of the company is at stake.
- I would report any irregularity in company finance.

Critics claim that job applicants are being put in an impossible position by such questions. If they play honest, they look disloyal to the company; if they play loyal, they are dishonest. Someone faced with such a test should insist on discussing it in detail with the personnel department and should point out its unacceptable implications. Looking for a job is not about incriminating yourself.

Honesty tests handle the problem I have highlighted. The tests covered in this chapter have their limits. Motivation and values are subtle qualities and most of the tests covered here, when you understand their design, can be answered in the way you think is wanted; the way that will suggest you are ambitious, energetic and really willing to work for the company. Only the warts you want to show will show if you are clever and subtle about it.

Tip seven. *If you are doing a computerized test, time yourself very accurately so you can scroll back to check your answers. Even tests that don't allow you to scroll forward allow you nearly always to scroll back. In the unlikely event that a computerized test doesn't allow this, politely ask why when you have finished.*

8. **Business games and role-playing**

You have just arrived in Aberdeen. You discover the regional sales manager of the Super Boot Corporation, your main rivals in selling specially reinforced boots for wear on oil rigs, has arrived in town. He has set up meetings with all your clients.

The man from Super Boot is more senior in his company than you are in yours. He has more authority to undercut prices and to offer special lines of credit. For anything over a standard 15 per cent discount, you have to get clearance from your regional office. Oil companies want to cut costs. All the companies fit out their workers with boots. If he manages to snatch 10 per cent of your clients, it will damage your company badly – and mean less commission for you. How do you respond to this crisis?

Conventional tests do not mirror this kind of real-life situation. Dealing with Super Boot's attempt to muscle in on your territory requires a mixture of aggression, intelligence, deviousness and tact. You might choose a number of strategies including:

The Casual Cool. When you see your clients, you mention you know he has been there and dangled discounts. But are his boots as good? Do they last as long? And if Super Boot were not in some kind of panic, would the high-powered regional sales manager come to Aberdeen?

The Measured Response. You offer to your clients to match any discounts your rival has offered. You know they are loyal customers. You don't want them to lose money because of their loyalty to a superior product. You hope you can get Head Office to wear it.

The Ostrich in Panic Response. You mention nothing to your regional office about Super Boot. Basically, you feel it reflects badly on you that Super Boot have targeted Aberdeen. They must know your clients are not very loyal. Really, they hate you. You act pathetic in front of clients and plead, rather like Willie Loman in Arthur Miller's famous play *Death of a Salesman*, for them to buy anything – anything at all. Your job is on the line.

The situation and the variety of possible responses (my three are just a crude sketch) show how much more complex real industrial situations are than the issues tests deal with. In an ideal world, what employers want to see is how people will react in situations that are like those on the job.

Attempts to test people in more realistic ways actually started during the 1939–45 war, when the British, American and German armies developed what are now called assessment centres in order to choose – and train – good officers. They put potential officers through tactical planning exercises and outdoor leadership exercises. These could include building bridges using ropes and pine logs, and organizing people to cross them. The tasks had to be done against the clock. If you could get your platoon across safely and in time, you would make it to lieutenant. If you failed, you remained a private. Experienced officers watched and judged.

The less military British Civil Service took up these ideas after the end of the war to decide who would make good senior civil servants. In the 1950s, a few leading companies also started to use these more realistic methods of assessment – and they have now become very fashionable for all but junior jobs.

Assessment centres also use role-playing and business games, terms that need to be defined. Nowhere else in this book have I discussed games or the ability to act. But, in a way, that is exactly what role-playing and business games require.

The techniques I describe in this chapter are used both in recruiting for certain jobs and, perhaps even more, in training and assessing how well you are doing once you have a job. Many large organizations send staff for annual appraisals so that they can monitor the progress of employees.

When a job is at stake, preparing for an assessment centre day is much like preparing for an interview. But it is a good idea to write to the employer beforehand and ask for some test examples so you can see how much work has to be done in the time limit. Assessment centres are extremely tiring, so get a good night's sleep the night before.

While it is stressful, a day at an assessment centre is also a great chance to outperform other candidates in front of an audience. There will often be team events and time to chat to employees and recent recruits. Such a day offers you an opportunity to find out more about the job, as well as for the employers to find out about you.

A word about team exercises which applies to all the tests covered in this chapter:

Team exercises

In team exercises, the most important thing is to work together to make sure you get a successful outcome. Not everyone can be a natural leader, so don't worry if someone is always trying to shout the loudest. Although being assertive does have some advantages, the assessors will, in theory at least, be experienced and know that the loudest person is not necessarily the most effective one.

TIP

If you are naturally quite shy, make sure you do make some contributions to the group discussions that are inevitably part of such a day. The person who never opens his or her mouth will seem odd.

EXERCISE

Again, you should list your strengths and weaknesses. I have made the list slightly longer than usual because the role-playing situation is unusual and many people will have absolutely no experience of it.

Strengths
- Have done amateur dramatics
- Think quickly on my feet

- Enjoy new situations
- Not shy
- Feel intrigued by this notion
- Grasp quickly what is wanted
- Good stamina
- Confident in groups
- Enjoy being away from home.

Weaknesses
- Hate groups
- Hate not having the time to prepare for new experiences
- Uncomfortable away from home
- Need lots of approval from whoever is in charge
- Find it hard to get on with new people
- Find it hard to speak in groups.

As these strengths and weaknesses suggest, to do well in role-playing games you need to be sharp, alert and have good social skills.

Don't despair. As usual, the more you know about it the better prepared you will be for meeting the needs of the occasion.

Assessment centre experience and exercises

There is no hard and fast rule for how assessment centres operate, but what follows is an outline of a day you might face. All professional assessment centres start by explaining how the day will run and introducing people to each other. This can be tense, because on the one hand you are supposed to work together with the others on group exercises, while on the other hand they are the competition.

General briefing	15 minutes
Verbal tests	30 minutes
Numerical tests	30 minutes
Break	15 minutes
Role-playing	
Briefing	15 minutes

Role-playing	45 minutes
Group discussion	45 minutes
Lunch	
Afternoon briefing	15 minutes
In-tray exercises	60 minutes
Job-specific tests	15 minutes
Business game	45 minutes
One-to-one feedback on your performance so far	30 minutes
End-of-day group discussion	30 minutes

This is a hard-working day and one where you need to be on your toes. We've already covered general, verbal and numerical tests. The assessment centre will be interested in seeing how you might deal with realistic situations.

If, for example, you are going for a manager's job in a supermarket, you are likely to be assessed on a day where you will have to deal with what will turn out to be routine tasks:

- working out what lines are selling and not selling
- making sure that the lines at checkouts do not get too long;
- ordering replacements of fast-selling goods in good time (stock control is a key variable in making a supermarket profitable)
- dealing with customer complaints
- making sure neither staff nor customers are stealing too much.

In the assessment centre, the assessors are typically looking for 'multiple competencies', as they are called. If someone is brilliant at working out what needs to be re-ordered but has a tendency to bark rudely at customers who complain, they may really not be the kind of person a supermarket wants to hire.

The general skills tested by assessment centres will include:

- written communication
- financial planning
- operational control
- service orientation

- perseverance
- networking.

All these exercises are fairly straightforward. The fun starts when you have to role-play.

The origins of role-playing

Role-playing is not a concept that originated in industry. It was first used in therapy. The idea was developed by a slightly eccentric psychoanalyst called Jacob Moreno. Moreno believed you could help people to conquer their complexities by getting them to act out situations they found especially difficult. He would first talk to his patients and find out what they saw as their key problems. Then, in a process called psychodrama, he would get them to act out with someone else these problematic scenes. The person they acted with was usually 'safe', usually another member of the therapy group.

Then Moreno would often get people to swop roles. If I have problems with my father because he is so ambitious for me Moreno would get me first to play myself; then I would play my father. The idea was to create a certain emotional liberation – drama has long been said to be cathartic – and also to give me some insight into how my father feels. Understanding what my father feels, why he wants me to be more ambitious, at least gives me some sense of his point of view. It makes me less egocentric and better able to deal with the conflict.

Moreno's ideas fit with an observation that sociologists were making in the 1950s. In some ways, they were seeing the obvious: we all act a great deal in our social lives; we wear masks; our true self is somewhere beneath the mask.

One famous study looked at hospital life. It found that doctors almost automatically take on a certain persona. They have authority: patients listen to them; nurses do what they say. If you ask a patient to take the part of a doctor, once they get into the swing of it, they begin to show all the characteristics typical of doctors. But they also start to see some of the dilemmas doctors face. How do you tell a patient who believes they are reasonably fit that they have an incurable cancer?

Psychodrama and role-playing can also be very effective

helping techniques because they allow people to rehearse how they will behave when it happens 'for real'.

I once made a film which followed a theatre group that toured prisons. One actress from the group, the Geese Theatre, told me that they gave inmates the chance to rehearse how they could deal with family crises. The inmates would get very tense when visiting day neared. They were not used to talking to women any more. Role-playing gave them the chance to rehearse with an actress how they would confront issues with their wives and girlfriends: 'Do you still love me?' 'Are you being unfaithful?'

Geese found that all these painful issues could be dealt with in group work. Role-playing can also be very funny, a release of all kinds of tensions.

In the 1970s, I co-produced a series of TV programmes called *Sex in Our Time*. We looked at how people reacted to members of the opposite sex. I organized a group of 12 men and women to spend a day playing role games. One involved the men playing women and the women playing men. The women had to chat the men up 'just like a man'. The men had to wait 'just like a woman'.

What was it like being in the shoes of the other sex? Often, very funny. Women who had to chat men up would dry up with embarrassment. Men couldn't bear not being the ones to take the initiative. The filming session intended that each would learn something of the experience of the other. Men would learn how women felt frustrated and helpless because it was (certainly in the 1970s) nearly always up to them to wait till the man made the first move. Women would learn that men found it hard to make that move and compensated sometimes by being too brash or aggressive. The film wasn't science but most people felt, by the end of the day, that they had got some useful insights.

Industry

Role-playing in industry started to be popular in the 1980s and for many of the same reasons. Such exercises make it possible to examine behaviour in some detail – and not always the behaviour you would expect. Business games are not just about seeing who has the smartest selling techniques.

Many of the business games I describe test how well people work together in groups. Often the mediator or leader will build in various constraints. The person who is leading the group has to change in mid-project. The style of leadership has to cope with such swapping of roles. It is expensive to put on a business game so they are more likely to be used with high-powered jobs than with 'ordinary' jobs. Probably the organization that has used some form of role-playing activity for longest in recruitment is the Civil Service. By the late 1960s, it was inviting potential high-flyers, who had done well in the Civil Service examinations created by Trevelyan (see chapter 1), to spend a few days in a country house under observation. The would-be bureaucrats would live together, eat together and role-play their responses to problems that blew up in the real world.

The kind of problems dealt with in such role-playing exercises might include how to deal with a new nuclear accident like Chernobyl or the possibility of a rise in interest rates. The fledgling bureaucrats and diplomats are observed – sometimes through one-way mirrors – as they react. Are they quick? Are they flexible? Do they respond to pressure well? Or does the fear that they have made a *faux pas* lead them to spill their soup over the wife of the Ecuadorian chargé d'affaires, which causes a new diplomatic incident and tension in the Pacific? More seriously, the format allows the Civil Service to judge how rigid the participants are and whether (which is crucial for diplomats) they turn out to be racists.

Trainers

The setting of such role-playing exercises can be strange and it is best to be prepared for it. You will be asked to go to somewhere like a hotel meeting room. There is likely to be a group of anything up to 20 people there. All the others in the group will be your rivals. If the game is part of the recruitment process, they will be your competitors for the job. If the game is part of the assessment and training process of the company you work for, they will be your peers (and rivals) in the company. All this takes a little getting used to, especially for people who have had no experience of anything like it before.

As I have argued throughout, one of the problems with tests is that many of them have not been well validated. At present there are a huge number of role-playing exercises around and we rather take it on trust that they work. Many of the trainers who work for particular companies make them up for specific tasks. I have selected here seven kinds of role-playing games that are widely used so that readers can get an idea of the variety of problems they may be asked to deal with. The games range from the fun to the highly realistic where people simulate events executives may have to deal with, often with time constraints built in.

Game One is about leadership and team building. The second game is about survival. The third game is about reacting to a crisis that has to be solved quickly and how a team operates under those pressures. The fourth game is about negotiation and communication, especially when dealing with foreign cultures. Game Five is about being confident in dealing with new technology. Game Six focuses on selling yourself in the selection process. Game Seven is the most realistic and is about creating and marketing a new product.

Those who use business games to recruit are often not very happy to talk about what they are doing. Part of the purpose of the role-playing exercises is to surprise people. In order not to be surprised and end up at a disadvantage, remember the following general rules.

TIPS

Tip one. *Be clear you know what is going on. You can ask questions before the game starts; once it is going, it is too late. You will be making yourself appear difficult because you will be interrupting the flow of the game. But, at the start, you have every right to know:*

- *What is the aim of the game?*
- *When does it end?*

- *What kind of feedback will I receive – and when?*
- *Is there a winner?*

Tip two. *No one will tell you how you are doing until the very end so do not seek reassurance. Part of the whole process is to see how you operate in the dark. Do not look to the trainer to help.*

Tip three. *Be pleasant. Those who observe games are often as interested in someone's personal style as in what they do. The ability to be co-operative, to both give and take leads is one thing you will be marked for.*

Tip four. *Encourage your colleagues where you can. That looks, and is, leadership.*

Tip five. *Never lose your temper. If you are in charge of a group, you may have to be angry but stay 'professionally' so.*

Each game I go on to describe has a different purpose and that means different tactics are likely to make you look good in it.

Game One: The Kite Game

Everyone wants individuals who are team players. Prima donnas are not attractive. One skill that business games can explore much better than ordinary tests is how well someone works with other members in the group.

The Kite Game tests team work on a simple task. The name of the game comes from its objective – to build a kite. The snag is that the group do not have the tools they need to make the kite; rather they have sticks, a black bag, string and no means to assemble them.

According to Rosemary Neal who runs training for many large companies, this game reveals much about who are the natural leaders in a group, who is good at coming up with solutions and getting the rest of the team to accept them, and how a team bonds. Technicians tend to become obsessed with small details.

TIP

If you have good practical intelligence, contribute lots of ideas but don't get upset or uptight if they don't work. Do not block the ideas of others. If you do not have good practical intelligence, own up and help the group by encouraging and by helping assess. Knowing your skills helps.

Game Two: The Balloon Game

Role-playing games also offer companies the chance to see how people react in more unreal situations and to more desperate crises than anything to do with a kite. The Balloon Game is psychologically very edgy, almost out of a Stephen King thriller.

The group have to pretend that they are in a balloon. The balloon is overloaded. The group has to vote on who next to throw out. You have to explain why you should not be the next one to take to the skies with no parachute. Do you do this by assuming leadership qualities – without you, no one will survive? Or do you do it by making yourself likeable? The game reveals the strategies people use under extreme pressure.

The game is, of course, very unrealistic and people know it. In Game One, there is a real kite to build. Here, all you do if you 'die' is lose face. According to some who have played, however, people often get very involved in it and the game becomes exceptionally bizarre when it is down to two people. Yes, under the rules, the balloon is still overcrowded. Someone has to bale out for the greater good.

The game does reveal a good deal about one's personality despite its lack of realism.

Executive exercises

In real businesses, people are not usually left to build the kite without the right equipment, or made to fly around in overloaded balloons. Many role-playing exercises are much more realistic and one that is sometimes used runs over a 12- to 24-hour basis through the night. You can see why people might find that attractive. If a real crisis blows up, people would need to work under just such pressures.

Game Three: Find the Deadly Chemical

This game reflects current concerns about the environment. It grew out of interest in developing management skills through outdoor and outward-bound groups. Fitness frenzy is booming; corporate gymnastics will allow you to abseil to greater profits and yomp to a greater market share.

Find the Deadly Chemical has to start late in the evening. The group is told that something toxic – a nuclear isotope, an oil drum of chemicals – has gone missing from their factory. They have to find it. Has it been stolen? By rival companies? By Greenpeace? Has it leaked? The organizers provide clues. The group has to decide who will look where. Often, it is an all-night job. A well-devised scenario will create many obstacles and pressures. Those who participate say that the night feels hard, long and real.

TIP

Stamina is essential. Do not, if you know it is going to be a long night, burn up all your energy at the beginning of the evening by having 50 good ideas and then feeling exhausted.

Three things will help your stamina: sheer determination not to flag; some tricks and treats; and keeping your focus on the goal.

Determination: *look at all your colleagues. Do you really want to be the first to flag? Old-fashioned will-power has its uses.*

Treats: *If you are going away on any kind of role-playing jaunt, take some treats. I would recommend a private supply of chocolate, of yoghurt-covered raisins and peanuts, a small bottle of eau de cologne and some fairly tart mouthwash. This may sound exotic but it is all designed to maintain stamina.*

Throughout the night, you can pep yourself up with chocolate and/or yoghurt raisins – plenty of energy in both. The privacy of the bathroom has its uses too. Disappear to brush your teeth and rinse your mouth out with your tart mouthwash. It is hard to feel sleepy if your mouth feels sharp.

Also stretch to keep your circulation going. Body rhythms slow down during the night so you need bursts of physical activity to keep alert.

Focus: *You need to visualize the objective of the night and your contribution to it. Give yourself the odd two or three minutes (and there is nearly always some quiet time) to visualize this.*

Do not look for the approval of the trainer or ask nervously if you are doing OK.

Game Four: Smile As You Drink Yak Soup

Executives have to be comfortable in dealing with people of very different cultures. British business needs exports but British attitudes can be xenophobic. Learning to love foreigners matters, however, in a world where you export – or die.

One nice game involves two teams negotiating a contract. One team is British, the other is from a different culture. The fun is that you do not have to deal with a real culture. Imaginative trainers get their groups to make up a bizarre culture – a process which can be fun. I have heard of groups in which there was the following set of rules:

- You have to negotiate sitting on the floor in the lotus position.
- You cannot say 'No'. In this culture, the use of the word 'No' is considered very rude.
- You have to appear to enjoy what seems to you strange food, such as yak soup. Remember that to someone from a different culture, sausages and beans may seem exotic and, indeed, disgusting.
- The culture is indecisive. What else would you expect of a culture that can't say 'No'? Yet through all this, you have to get the deal because it is desperately important for your cash-starved company.

The aim of the exercise is to see how flexible you are and how able to accept 'foreign' ways. Increasingly, British business needs to be export-oriented. I once very nearly lost a deal because I did not raise my glass to be filled with Saki, though, luckily, that cultural error was forgotten as drinking progressed through the evening.

TIP

Use humour; not humour that pokes fun at the other culture but at your own initial clumsy attempts to cope with it. Being able to laugh at yourself suggests confidence and an ability to cope in odd situations without getting flummoxed.

Game Five: New Technology

Game Five focuses on the fact that businesses increasingly change the technologies they use and require employees to be very flexible. In the next game, you have to devise a simple computer program. The company instals chocolates, snacks and soft drinks in vending machines. You need a program that will tell you when you need to restock those vending machines. The problem involves a mixture of common sense, some mathematics and a willingness to work out the logical steps on a computer that will say when the machines need to be filled again.

TIP

The question is basically a logical one. Much of the advice I gave on dealing with New Technology Tests in the last chapter applies.

Game Six: The Whitehall Game

Many companies find it well worthwhile to adapt one of the two-day interview formats which the Civil Service use. Unlike the majority of role-playing games, which are deliberately set in a neutral, artificial space, here candidates have to spend anything from 24 to over 48 hours at a hotel or country house. They are away from it all and, of course, it is artificial but not entirely so. People eat together and have some spare time to socialize together.

The heart of the exercise is usually a set of scenarios which the participants have to deal with. In a complicated exercise like this, some of them will be individual set pieces. The Chairperson wants to know how to react tomorrow when the *Financial Times* interviews him or her about the closure of a factory in Newcastle. How can he or she justify that?

Other scenarios will involve the whole group. The group

will be set a marketing problem such as how to revamp a well-established product. Should the product be changed? Or is all that needs to change the marketing, advertising and distribution?

The exercise may be completely free-wheeling; everyone can pitch in with ideas. Or it may be highly structured. The night before, you may be given a brief in which you are head of design or head of production or head of marketing. You will then have to speak for your department. Some of the problems to solve will be group problems.

Remember, your performance will be minutely observed. In some situations companies use one-way mirrors and may well video the whole game. The process tests flexibility under pressure, the ability to work both by oneself and with others.

TIP

Within limits, be yourself. If you try to play a different type, you are likely to appear inconsistent. Specific hints:

- *Don't talk too much.*
- *When you speak, keep it short and to the point.*
- *Resist the temptation to score off the others.*
- *If the game splits you into two groups, then you can show aggressive humour against the other team.*
- *Make lots of eye contact with your colleagues but don't keep looking at the trainer for approval. That suggests insecurity.*

Game Seven: Making Novelties

Over 12 hours, a group has to create a product, design it, decide how to market it and sell it. It is a very advanced version of the Kite Game. Sometimes children from local schools are brought in to be either the potential customers or the sales force. Good businesses often try to involve the community. This game is realistic and can have unexpected benefits. In one case, a group was asked to design and build an adventure playground for handicapped children. The group then went on to do that for real. This close-to-reality simulation draws together many of the skills tested in other games.

Debriefing

A crucial part of role-playing is debriefing. You have the right to know how you did and what you did wrong, so insist that you get something out of this exercise. It may not be praise; it may just be a greater awareness of your weaknesses, which gives you something useful to work on in the future. If the trainer does not offer a proper debrief, ask for one for yourself and one for the group.

There are signs of revolt against some of these procedures. An article by Dr E. Clunes of the University of Nottingham pointed out that many managers in the Health Service did not see why it took three days of testing, role-playing and interviews to choose who would get a job. High-flying executives can take that stand. Most of us, however, cannot. Therefore getting comfortable with such games is very useful for executives of all grades. All the evidence suggests that they will be used more and more in industry in the future.

9. **Practice makes perfect**

At the start of this book, I argued that the more you understand your strengths and weaknesses, the better your chance of doing well in job hunting – and much else beside. Analysis should lead to action. In this chapter, I want to draw together the themes of this book so that you can devise an individual progress plan. You first need to look at how you did on the anxiety test.

Anxiety answers

You were told that you did not have to tick just one answer to each question. There is a letter marked against each answer.

Q1 aC bA cA dA eC fL
Q2 aC bB cL dA
Q3 aA bC cA dA
Q4 aC bB cC dB
Q5 aC bB cC dA eA
Q6 aC bB cL dL
Q7 aC bB cL dA
Q8 aL bB cL dA
Q9 aL bB cB
Q10 aA bC cB dc
Q11 aA bL cB dL eC
Q12 aB bC cA
Q13 Score 1A for any tick to a, b, c, d.
Q14 aB bC cA

Tot up the number of As, Ls, Bs and Cs you have scored. A stands for Anxiety, B for Balance, L for Luck, C for Cockiness. The total possible score is As: 19; Bs: 13; Ls: 10; Cs: 13.

This test does not pretend to have gone through the quality control procedure tests should have gone through, but it does provide a rough and ready guide to your reactions to situations in which you need to prove yourself. I have divided the responses to each question into four basic tendencies.

Anxiety. Every point that you score here suggests you are anxious about doing tests and about how you present yourself. You feel very responsible for yourself but sometimes you are annoyed that you do not feel in control of your responses.

Luck. Every point that you score here suggests that you attribute success or failure not to yourself but to outside forces. Your fate is in the stars not in the way that you behave. You could be said to be unrealistic. One theory divides people into those who have an inner locus of control and those who have an outer locus of control. To believe so much in luck is to have an outer locus of control.

Balance. Each point here suggests a sensible attitude. But are you really telling the truth about what you feel and how you act? There is nothing to be learned from this test if you are going to fake because here the only audience is yourself.

Cockiness. Each point here suggests that you tend to be too confident. One problem with my test should by now be evident. Those who are vastly over-confident may not actually tick many of those items. They may not think that they are cocky at all but believe they are balanced, and careful in how they approach tests.

I designed the test to bring out these factors because much research on responses to specific tests suggests that each type represents a common attitude.

How to handle anxiety

There is nothing spectacular about the advice for the over-anxious. You need to relax, you need to persuade yourself that your whole life does not depend on how you do on a particular test and the associated interview. Here are some specific techniques.

- Try very hard to learn to relax through deep breathing and clearing your mind. If you find that you have obsessive thoughts of failure, dream up another scenario. You will be convinced by an easy fantasy of success so use the detailed mental rehearsal outlined in chapter 2 to take yourself through all the stages of job application and selection.
- Be well prepared. Give yourself plenty of time to get to the place where you are going for the test. If you are relying on public transport, remember trains and buses are always late when you really need them. Locate the place on a map. Freud claimed that our unconscious mind plays tricks on us. If you are really anxious about how well you will do at an interview, one way of making sure you don't really fail is not to get there at all. If you don't get there, no one can test you so you cannot fail. Brilliant! Find your destination on an A to Z the day before and leave early. It may be smart to be a little late for parties or for power meetings but it is wise to be a little early for job applications.
- Familiarize yourself with the kinds of questions, puzzles and games you may find yourself set. That is why I recommend doing puzzles in puzzle magazines. Academic psychologists may dismiss these as trivial but they are fairly similar to items in many tests.
- Keep a sense of perspective about the whole process. This is not easy. We all need work and we want to prove ourselves, but there will always be other jobs to go for.
- If you feel you are very deficient in some skills – if, for example, you know that you spell poorly because you weren't taught well at school – seek out a specific remedial course. Local authorities run plenty of them and Job Centres have information about some of them.

Luck

The problem for those who tick many L responses is essentially one of attitude. You tend to think that you deserve neither success nor failure when you meet either of them. There is no doubt that life isn't fair and that, sometimes, people get jobs for no good reason. Someone may take a fancy – even in these politically correct days – to a 'leggy blonde' or to a young man who just happens also to be an Arsenal supporter. You cannot do anything about that, but there is a lot that you can do something about. A book like this cannot hope to change your fundamental attitudes, but if you have ticked many answers that indicate luck, you should think whether this is really what you feel or whether it is a comforting story you tell yourself because you are so frightened of failure.

Balance

In theory your attitude to tests is sensible. The main thing you should ask yourself is whether you have answered the questions honestly and whether that really is how you behave in testing situations.

Cockiness

In some ways this is the hardest of all tendencies to overcome – and I know because I am personally a little inclined to it. The best advice that one can give is that over-confident people tend to do tests too quickly and, in IQ-like tests, to make careless mistakes. This is especially true with numerical questions.

- Try not to be careless.
- Check your answers.
- Restrain yourself from too silly answers in creativity tests.
- In attitude tests which use five-point or seven-point scales, don't mark too many extremes.

  These 'profiles' are very general. I suspect many of us know what we do wrong in such situations. The point is to face that and decide to change.

The Balance Sheet of the Self

John Watson's idea of the Balance Sheet of the Self was based on a simple idea. You cannot hope to use psychology to change yourself and improve your life chances unless you look honestly at your strengths and weaknesses. The more you understand about yourself, the better your hopes of equipping yourself for job hunting.

You should have filled in this balance sheet at the start of chapter 2. The idea of the balance sheet is straightforward: it is an attempt to get you to rate your current strengths and weaknesses. If there are any headings you do not understand, leave them blank now and try to fill them in after reading the relevant chapter.

Each Quality has two pairs of columns divided by a column for 'Action and time span'. The first of each pair is for your Rating; the second is for how you feel about it.

Rate yourself on a scale of 1 to 10 on each skill, where 10 is total mastery; 7 is good; 5 is average; 3 is poor; and 1 is very poor.

The feelings I suggest you put in the box are either Satisfied, Want to improve, Don't think it matters, or, Anxious about it.

Psychologists use a lot of self-report but it is a good idea to show your balance sheet to your partner or someone you trust to see if they disagree wildly with your self-assessment. This is perhaps risky but, especially if you have a tendency either to anxiety or over-confidence, some external check is useful.

Having assessed your state at the start of this process, you should note in the middle row if you are going to take action and what action you are going to take. Then you can go back to see how you have done.

Quality	Self-rating	Feeling	Acton & time-span	Self-rating	Feeling
Intelligence					
Verbal skills					
Vocabulary					
Wide reading					
Synonym skills					
Opposite word skills					
Rhyming					
Number of word associations					
Speed of word associations					
Spelling check					
Anagrams					
Crossword puzzle skills					
Alphabet					
Number skills					
Basic addition					
Basic division					
Basic subtraction					
Basic multiplication					
Fractions					

Sequence skills

Converting letters
into numbers

Spatial skills

Easily grasp
figure puzzles

Changed objects

Closure skills

Practical skills

Break practical
problems into
chunks easily

Mechanically
competent

Fear of technology

Computer literate

Confused by
programming

Special skills

Music

Art

Personality

Sociable

Stable

Good at dealing with
difficult people

Shy

Level of anxiety

Attribution of
control

Honest

Temper

Tendency to anger

Tendency to panic

Self-control

Skilled in groups

Frightened of groups

High neurotic score

Low self-esteem

Recent life changes

Easily stressed

General social skills

Creativity

Fluency of ideas

Critical assessment

Fear of
looking foolish

Attitude

Clear goals

Drive

Stamina

Persistence

Often careless

Fear of failure

Fear of success

Never know what
to say to people

Fear of criticism

Constructive in use
of criticism

Secret failings

Any other remarks*

---

* Here you should particularly note what motivates you.

You should count anything you rate 7 or above as a Fundamental Strength; anything 3 or below as a Fundamental Weakness.

The easiest skills to build up will probably be the ones you rate 5 or average but you probably also need to grit your teeth and deal with Fundamental Weaknesses.

- List your *Fundamental Strengths*.
- List your *Fundamental Weaknesses*.
- Choose which 'Average' skills you will work on.

Time-span

The clearer the goal and the time frame, the easier it will be for you to improve your performance. So choose the three things you most want to work on and decide how long you will work on them: 1 week, 1 month, 3 months, long-term goal.

Having identified what areas you want to work on, you need to consider how best to organize your efforts.

Practice effects

The orthodox psychological view is that practice and rehearsal can do little to help improve test scores. Academic books on testing devote surprisingly little space to the effects of practice. The authoritative *Psychological Testing and Assessment* squeezes all that we know about coaching and practice into one and a half of its 594 pages.

In fact, much evidence suggests practice can improve scores on those tests where it makes sense to talk of 'improving', like IQ and creativity tests. You cannot improve your score on a personality test. At most you can learn to fake more convincingly.

Remember the origins of IQ. I pointed out at the start of this book that IQ tests came out of work by French psychologists which aimed to boost children's school performance. In the 1960s, America started programmes like Headstart for poor children, which gave them access to more toys, better nursery care, better food and a positive attitude to learning. There is no doubt that children who went through Headstart initially did better at school, though some psychologists claim it was not because they had a higher IQ but because they were motivated.

Rehearsing IQ

Psychologists who are sceptical about programmes like Headstart argue that intelligence is largely inherited. It may be possible to slightly change the IQ of a child by providing a very stimulating environment but, after the age of eight, it is just too late.

There has been much less research on whether the IQ of adults can change. The evidence there is suggests modest improvements are possible. One study in the 1960s looked at the effect of six hours' intensive coaching. On average, people who went through that coaching scored a nine-point IQ rise – nothing to make a nitwit into a genius but quite enough to boost your chances of getting a job.

The most detailed research into the effects of coaching and practice on adults has come from North America. In the USA, tests very similar to IQ tests, called SAT (School Assessment Test), are taken by high school graduates who want to go to college. Most people who take the SAT are 17, 18 or 19. Your score on the SAT is all important. The SAT includes one test for verbal and one for mathematical skills. Your score decides whether you go to college and which college you will go to. So parents want their children to do well on SATs. Cramming and coaching institutions do good business claiming they will transform mediocre Johnny into a high SAT scorer.

In 1971, the College Examination Board said that there was no point in parents wasting good dollars on sending their children to intensive cramming. The SAT, being like an IQ test, was not something you could practise for.

One of the many test coaching organizations challenged this negative finding. Stanley H. Kaplan, who headed the largest test coaching organization in the USA, questioned the basis of the research. In 1979, the Federal Trade Commission released the results of a ten-week coaching period at one of Kaplan's institutions. They concluded that verbal and mathematical skills could be improved by coaching. Kaplan seemed to have won, but that was not the end of the controversy.

Psychologists who examined the Federal Trade Commission study were not convinced. They declared that the SATs were not good predictors of performance in college and that they did not test the capacity to learn. Any comparison with an IQ test was mistaken. IQ cannot be learned.

By now, reputations were at stake. In America, there is also a prestigious Educational Testing Service which helps devise tests and advises on government policy. They reassessed the coaching study. They found the results were strange. There were differences between various of the schools Kaplan directed. In two schools, coaching seemed to produce just small increases in performance. In a third school, students showed a hefty rise of between 20 and 35 points on both verbal and mathematical items. (It is not possible to translate SAT scores easily into IQ scores but the rise was significant.)

After this statistical saga and many studies, the received wisdom is that you can boost SAT scores but it takes a lot of doing. About 45 hours of coaching can lead to a boost of between eight and 12 points; 200 hours of coaching can lead to a bigger boost of 30 points. But what exactly do you concentrate on?

EXERCISES

The kind of exercises you need to do to boost your IQ performance will depend critically on what you are good at and what you are bad at.

Verbal skills

- Wordplay. Building up your vocabulary and improving your synonym/opposite word skills can be done at the same time. Note down 15 words every day. Find for each of these 15 words two words that mean the same and two words that are the opposite. This shouldn't take too much time but can get you juggling with language.
- Do anagrams. The easiest way is to select words of between six and eight letters, e.g. BOOSTER, REACTING, VARIOUS, BURNED, and see how many other words you can make out of them. Give yourself a time limit like ten minutes.
- A good book to dip into if you want to go on a dazzling tour of words is *Roget's Thesaurus*. Much of it is a bit antiquated now but a five-minute dip will certainly boost your word power.

- Do crosswords because again they give you the chance to juggle words and a bit of logic.
- It is harder to improve your numerical skills in a fun way. You either can or can't treat maths as a game. The main skill you can learn through practice is to analyse sequences so that the sequence questions get easier.
- Get very familiar with the alphabet because so many questions ask you to replace letters with numbers or vice versa.
- Practice Sudoku.

Spatial skills

- Analyse visual puzzles into chunks.
- Learn to look at visual puzzles from different angles.
- Practise abstracting key elements, so that you can focus on just what is crucial. This is essentially breaking puzzles down into chunks.

Organization skills

- If you really want to boost your performance, be disciplined in how you approach improving your skills. You can write out an extended balance sheet to monitor progress over months.
- You need to practise and, essentially, that means getting hold of more tests. There are reputable books, like Eysenck's, which offer exercises. But I also recommend puzzle magazines because they do demand a certain playfulness and they do offer a constant diet of brain teasers.

If practice works, it raises questions. Are students doing better because the practice has made them more intelligent? Or has the practice made them more confident? Or more motivated? Theoretically, the question is fascinating; practically, it is irrelevant. SAT scores have been shown to get better.

The kind of research already referred to on p. 140 irritates some psychologists because, in a way, they make tests seem less reliable. But the lesson is plain. Practice will not turn a village idiot into a physicist but you can certainly benefit from getting familiar with questions like those you will meet in tests.

Learning for other tests

More surprising is that some very simple skills you would think are basic and biological also improve with practice. The Digit Span task is the most obvious.

I have to confess the question of whether practice improves performance in one kind of testing particularly intrigues me. Do people get better on creativity tests the more they do them? It is hard not to believe the more you do the Uses of Objects or the Remote Associates Test the better you will get at them – and there is some research on bright children who did the Uses of Objects that supports that. But there is less research on creativity than on IQ, so it is hard to be sure.

Creativity practice

This is harder to practice for than IQ but again it is possible to think up some exercises.

- Practise devising puns. Even the ghastliest *Carry On* film puns make you see improbable verbal connections; they flex the pathways of the brain – exactly what you want both for the Uses of Objects test and the Remote Associates Test.
- Rhymes. Test how many rhyming words of at least five letters and more you can find for words. Some easy words: GAIN, RACE, PURSE. Move on to harder words like RIPPLE, SERENE and ASYLUM.
- Try to devise questions for the Remote Associates Test.

In-tray exercises

The more senior the job you are going for the more likely you are to be faced by these. A good way to prepare is to think of the ten most difficult problems you've had to deal with in the last 12 months. Write these down in no more than four sentences each. Then think of why you arrived at the solution you did and of alternative solutions. Practise seeing alternatives so no solution on paper will flummox you.

Personality and attitude tests

These are much harder to train for. The essential things you can do are:

- Remember the risks of 'faking good'.
- Watch out for items that invite you to exaggerate your virtues.
- Don't lie about qualifications or anything else that can be checked.
- On Inkblots or Projective Tests, like TAT, usually try to find responses that suggest drive, ambition, a highly motivated individual.
- Practice on all tests – IQ, creativity and personality – may also help just by making you feel more confident about the whole process.

TIP

This is very obvious but don't cheat yourself. If you are going to practise, get a book of IQ tests by a reputable author like Eysenck and buy a new copy. Copies in libraries tend to have some of the answers scribbled in in pencil. That is great for making you feel you are doing better than you really are.

You should by now have a whole range of aids to help you analyse your strengths and weaknesses and work on them. You can make or get extra copies of the Balance Sheet of the Self which allow you to track progress over months.

Do tests predict success?

Some tests are mere hype, as I hope by now to have illustrated. The best validated tests like the IQ tests and the personality tests devised by Eysenck and Cattell are far from useless but it is less easy to be sure just what they are useful for.

Even the most fervent, reputable advocates of testing are careful in their claims. The most that someone like Cattell or

Eysenck has ever claimed is that a high level of IQ or a high level of extroversion correlates with success in various fields.

Correlation is a tricky statistical concept but vital if you want to understand what tests can and cannot predict. A correlation is not a cause. If I play billiards and I hit ball A so that it hits ball B which goes into the pot, you could say that ball A *caused* ball B to land in the pot.

Few things in human sciences are so simple. Most psychological findings show correlations between A and behaviour B. Let us say that B is being a good pilot, one who manages to take off, understands what air traffic control is saying and doesn't land in Moscow thinking it's Glasgow.

Being a good pilot correlates with IQ. That means that on the whole good pilots will tend to have a high IQ score. It does not mean that all good pilots will have a high IQ score or that having a high IQ causes you to be a good pilot.

Correlations are expressed numerically. A correlation of 1 would be perfect. If every good pilot had an IQ of over 125, then there would be a perfect fit between being a good pilot and having an IQ of 125. (There almost certainly is a perfect 1 correlation between being a good pilot and having an IQ over 80 because someone with an IQ lower than that just could not master the numerical and performance skills you need to fly.)

A correlation of 0 states that there is no relationship between one thing and another. This would not mean that no pilot was intelligent but it was pure fluke whether any pilot you tested happened to have an IQ of 125 or higher, or a lower IQ.

A positive correlation of 0.7 is very high. In terms of job success, psychologists reckon that a correlation of 0.3 is meaningful and worth pursuing.

Not only is the concept of correlation statistically tricky but it's also intellectually complicated. First, how do you rate success? And perhaps more critical, who rates it?

In one study of 10,000 employees, the factor used to judge success was how their supervisor rated them. You do not have to be paranoid to see that this wasn't wholly objective. Are supervisors always fair? How much do they know? Are they not more likely to rate you as a success if they like you? What happens if they were the person who hired you in the first place? Usually, they will want to show they were right. Of course you're a success! What happens if you get up their nose? You're lousy.

Increasingly, employers are building more objective assessments into their personnel procedures because they know these pitfalls. But being objective is not always easy. Take a case that looks simple. Surely the better salesperson is the one who brings in more sales? Are you sure?

John H. and Flora B. are both reps for a large company which sells greeting cards. They manage to put in fairly comparable figures. John works the South East of England where there is still more money than in the North; Flora works Edinburgh, Newcastle and Glasgow.

Flora has a hard time. First, she has to face competition from Scottish card companies who produce cards of men in kilts drinking whisky of the Isles while balancing a caber. Many Scottish shops feel a certain national pride and stock these cards which are often bought by tourists. Second, some Northern areas are poorer. So the shops Flora visits put in smaller orders. For her to achieve the same sales figures as John is a triumph. The objective figures would not tell you that.

Then, there are jobs such as teaching or being a doctor where it is really a struggle to find any objective criteria of success. Is a good teacher one who crams his or her students well so that they pass exams or one who instils in them a love of learning they will have for the rest of their lives? These are impossible questions to answer.

It is as well to remember these problems whatever results you get on tests. If you do well, it doesn't make you a total hero. If you do badly, you shouldn't despair.

For personnel officers, it is as well to be aware of the controversies about how to define success and to think clearly about how to measure success in various jobs.

Final verdict

There will never be a final verdict on how good tests are, because tests are changing – in some ways improving – and the job environment is also changing. The following modest conclusions are true:

- Industry will continue to use tests. They are here to stay.
- IQ tests are modestly useful in general and if they are sensibly used they can be of considerable use in matching people to some jobs.
- The well-established personality tests like those of Eysenck and Cattell do reveal something about personality traits. From an occupational point of view, they are probably most use in revealing the kind of anxiety that is a major handicap in some jobs.
- The mix of intelligence and personality testing that the full-scale Cattell test offers can be of great use to large companies who want to decide not just whether to recruit someone but what kind of job to give them.
- Creativity tests can be fun and can reveal, at least, people who find the process worrying.
- There is a good body of evidence to back up the value of tests of drive like the Hilson and the TAT tests.
- Personnel departments and anyone who buys tests to use in selection should beware of eccentric tests and those which come with too positive claims of what they can achieve without very detailed and comprehensive research references to back them up.
- Throughout the book, in commenting on particular tests, I have tried hard to emphasize the limits of testing. Even the well-established tests are limited. A correlation of 0.7 between verbal skills and getting a job in journalism suggests that there are plenty of people in journalism who are doing well without any verbal skills at all.
- It is important for those who run testing to make sure that the people who are being tested are as comfortable and unanxious as possible. Try to put them at ease. Ask them if anything about the testing process scares them.
- If you are being tested, remember the ways best suited to you for handling anxiety.

Given how unreliable interviewing is, tests have a useful role to play in selection and assessment but no one should rely just on test scores in deciding whether or not to hire someone or where to place them in a large firm. Factors just as important are:

– their previous track record;
– what they have to say for themselves at interview;
– what they say about how they felt about the tests when they took them. The value of tests is enhanced by sensitive and intelligent interpretation of tests.

For those who have to take tests, there is one final issue. How to deal with success and/or failure.

10. **Success and failure**

I once met a man on the Eurostar who explained to me that he had been a leading headhunter and that he had appointed Greg Dyke to be director general of the BBC. But after this triumph he had decided that his true mission in life was selling umbrellas. I have no idea whether he was telling the truth or was a fantasist, but let's assume he was telling the truth. He was obviously a top headhunter, but something drove him to do something rather more eccentric. Thank God we are eccentric – and there is a lesson there both for people and for the recruiting industry. Incidentally, if there is a test which will reveal whether you will be an ace umbrella salesman, I have yet to identify it.

This shows how issues surrounding psychometric testing matter now that there are international conferences at which test-makers pool information and insights. What especially worries the professionals is the question of how to translate tests properly so that what works in Chicago can also work in China.

As I come to the end of writing this book, there's one important message about triumph and disaster. Rudyard Kipling's famous poem 'If' has the following lines:

If you can dream – and not make dreams your master;
If you can think – and not make thoughts your aim;
If you can meet with Triumph and Disaster
And treat those two impostors just the same;

The message was clear: a real man – in those pre-feminist days no one considered women – knew how to deal with either triumph or disaster. Both were impostors.

It is not easy to be quite so detached about getting work. But Kipling had a point. Work is only part of life. You shouldn't allow either success or failure to affect you too much.

That's easy if you have work. Getting a job always means new problems. Office life can be full of stresses and rivalries, but you are in and you have every reason to feel good about yourself. If you keep your balance sheet, you'll be able to monitor your progress on the job.

It is much harder to keep things in perspective if you fail to get jobs. The main problem that repeated failure brings is a sense of helplessness. It seems that there is nothing you can do to get work. You are not in control of your fate. For many people, that makes them feel both guilty and anxious.

It is easy to understand why failing to get work should make you feel guilty and anxious but these are not appropriate reactions. In a recession, getting work is never easy. Keep that in mind and use the techniques to deal with anxiety outlined in chapter 2.

You need to keep your failures in perspective and not to be too hard on yourself. You also need to take action to change. The key point is to work out why companies are rejecting you.

- Is it to do with your lack of qualifications?
- Is it to do with your performance at interview?
- Is it to do with the way you present yourself?
- Is it to do with the way you perform on tests?

Try to get personnel departments to give you some indication of why you failed to come up to scratch. You can do something about each of these failings. The balance sheet allows you to identify your weaknesses.

Taking some sort of definite action will have two benefits. First, and this is psychologically important, you will feel that you are taking control of your fate; you won't feel quite so helpless. Second, the skills you develop should make you more attractive to companies.

By working on your skills, you will feel less helpless and more in control of your own destiny, which will make you more confident and feel better about yourself. That is the frame of mind you want to be in when you set out job hunting again.

Solution to Sudoku puzzle in chapter 4, p. 54.

4	2	7	9	6	8	3	5	1
8	1	3	2	5	4	6	7	9
6	9	5	7	1	3	4	2	8
1	6	9	8	2	5	7	4	3
5	7	4	1	3	9	2	8	6
2	3	8	6	4	7	1	9	5
3	5	2	4	8	6	9	1	7
7	8	1	3	9	2	5	6	4
9	4	6	5	7	1	8	3	2

Useful addresses

UK

British Psychological Society
St Andrew's House
48 Princess Road East
Leicester LEI 7DR
Tel.: 0116 254 9568
Fax: 0116 227 1314
Website: www.bps.org.uk
Email: enquiry@bps.org.uk

Chartered Institute of Personnel and Development
151 The Broadway
London SW19 1JQ
Tel.: 020 8612 6200
Website: www.cipd.co.uk

Department for Innovation, Universities and Skills
Sanctuary Buildings
Great Smith Street
London SW1P 3BT
Tel.: 0870 000 2288
Enquiry line: 0870 001 0336
Fax: 01928 794248
Website: www.dfes.gov.uk

USA

American Psychological Association
750 First Street, NE
Washington
DC 20002-4242
USA

Tel.: 001 800 374-2721 or 001 202 336-5500
Website: www.apa.org

US Department of Labor

Frances Perkins Buildings
200 Constitution Avenue, NW
Washington
DC 20210
USA
Tel.: 001 866 4 USA DOL
Website: www.dol.gov

Index

accuracy tests 35–6
Ali, Muhammad 43, 61
American Psychological
    Association 17
Assessment Centres 117–19
Atkinson R. 103

Balance Sheet of the Self
    26, 37, 134–9
Bartram, D. 4–5
Baxter, J. 10
Binet, Alfred 11, 41–2
British Psychological
    Society 2, 3, 17–21, 105
business games 114

Cattell, R. 71, 73, 147
Cattell 16PF Scale 73
Churchill, W. 9–10
Clunes, E. 129
Columbia Driver
    Judgment Test 14–15
convergent/divergent
    thinking 44, 88–93
Cosell, H. 61
creativity tests 147

De Bono, E. 88, 95–7
decision analysis test 6, 67
Dickens, Charles 88
Digit Span 50
Drake, Francis 103

Einstein, A. 9–10
Eliot, T. S, 79
Eysenck, H. 10, 17,
    71–6, 142, 144, 147

Freud, S., 85, 132
Fox, G. 44

Galton, F. 38–40
Gardner, H. 58
GMA Test 6, 63–7
Guildford, J. P. 89

Headstart 139

Hemery, D. 32
Hilson Personality Profile
    81–3, 84
history of IQ 38–40
Hogan Personality
    Inventory 83

Industrial Relations Service
    1
Intelligence Tests 37–68,
    139
    numerical skills 50–3
    organization skills 142
    practical skills 57–8
    spatial skill, 54–6, 142
    verbal skills 46–50, 141
internet and testing 4–5
in-tray exercises 59–60,
    143
Impara, J. C. 12

Jung, C. J. 78–80

Kaplan, S. 140
Kipling, R. 149
Kline, P. 48

Long Term Credit 10
Lynn, R. 41–2

McClelland, D. 103–4
Mensa 10
mental imagery 32–4
Miller, A. 115
Moore, R. 7, 43–4
Moreno, J. 119
Morrisby Differential Test
    Battery 71–2
Murphy, K. 82–3
Myers Briggs test 6, 78–81

nAch (need for
    achievement) 102–3
Neal, R. 120

Odams 71
Ornstein, R. 58

personality tests 144
Plake, B. 12
projective tests 100–2
Psychological Corporation,
    the 11, 24

Reed Consulting 5
Remote Associates test 93
Report on Police Integrity 6
role playing 119–28
Rorschach test 15, 101–2,
    105
Rushton, P. 61

Sailer, S. 41–2
School Assessment Tests,
    140–1
Shelley, D. 16, 72
Simon, T. 11, 40–1
Skills Inventory for Teams
    111
Smithers, A. 71
Spielrein, S. 80
Spies, C. 12
Sternberg, R. 58
Strong Interest Inventory
    108
Sudoko 54

TAT test 102–3, 105
Tolkien, J. R. R. 103
Torrance Test of Creative
    Thinking 94
Trevelyan, C. 8–9, 121

Varhanen, T. 41–2

Watson, J. B. 24, 134
Wechsler Scale 46, 74
Wodehouse, P. G. 42

Yerkes Dodson Law 29–31

David Cohen **How to Succeed in Psychometric Tests**

Third edition

First published in Great Britain 1993

Sheldon Press
36 Causton Street
London SW1P 4ST

Second edition published 1999
Third edition published 2007

British Library Cataloguing-in-Publication Data
A catalogue record for this book is available from the British
Library

ISBN 978–1–84709–000–3

3 5 7 9 10 8 6 4 2

Typeset by Deltatype Ltd, Birkenhead, Merseyside
Printed in Great Britain by Ashford Colour Press

Produced on paper from sustainable forests